BUYING AND CONTRACTING FOR RESOURCES AND SERVICES

A How-To-Do-It Manual for Librarians

Rick Anderson

**HOW-TO-DO-IT MANUALS
FOR LIBRARIANS**

NUMBER 125

NEAL–SCHUMAN PUBLISHERS, INC.
New York, London

Published by Neal-Schuman Publishers, Inc.
100 William Street, Suite 2004
New York, NY 10038

The paper used in this publication meets the minimum require-
ments of American National Standard for Informational Sciences—
Permanence of Paper for Printed Library Materials, ANSI
Z39.48—1992⊖

Printed and bound in the United States of America.

Library of Congress Cataloging-in-Publication Data

Anderson, Rick, 1965–
    Buying and contracting for resources and services: a how-to-
do-it manual for librarians / Rick Anderson.
            p. cm.—(How-to-do-it manuals for librarians; no. 125)
    Includes index.
    ISBN 1-55570-480-8 (alk. paper)
    1. Acquisitions (Libraries)—Management. 2. Libraries and
booksellers. 3. Libraries and publishing. 4. Library materials—
Purchasing—Management. 5. Library fittings and supplies—
Purchasing—Management. 6. Contracts. 7. Negotiation in business.
I. Title. II. How-to-do-it manuals for libraries: no. 125.

Z689.A65 2004
025.2—dc22
                                            2003056204

DEDICATION

This book is lovingly dedicated to my wife Laura and to our beautiful and goofy children Maggie, Bryan, and Tucker.

CONTENTS

Foreword ix
Preface xi
Acknowledgments xix

I. Learning The Essentials Of Vendor Relations

Chapter 1   **Working With Vendors: The State Of The Art** 3
It Is The Best Of Times, It Is The Worst Of Times 3
New Library Tasks For The Online World 4
It's Still The Wild, Wild Web 7

Chapter 2   **Being A Good Customer** .9
The Customer Is Not Always Right 9
How To Be A Squeaky Wheel 9
If You Act Like A Jerk, You Will Look Incompetent 12

Chapter 3   **Getting Off On The Right Foot** 13
Say Your Name 13
Know The Lingo 14
The Heartbreak Of Jargon 15
Assume Good Faith   .16
Return Messages Promptly And Professionally 17
Be Assertive But Reasonable 18

II. Establishing Successful Vendor Relations

Chapter 4   **Issuing A Request For Proposals** 21
Be Careful What You Wish For 21
Give Them Time And Let Them Negotiate 22
Be A Good Host 23
After The Presentation 24

Chapter 5   **Establishing A New Service** 27
Someone Must Be In Charge 27
Settle Your Internal Arguments Beforehand 28

Know What You Want And What Is Available 28

Pre-Visit Checklist 29

Set An Agenda And Stick To It 31

Beyond Controlling The Schedule 32

Build A Shared Vocabulary 32

Introduce, Introduce, Introduce 34

Chapter 6 **Negotiating Terms Of Service** **37**

Discounts And Service Fees 37

Status Reports And Cancellations 41

Arranging Payment 41

Returns 44

Chapter 7 **Negotiating A License Agreement** **45**

Why You Need To Pay Attention To License Agreements 45

Three Categories Of License Terms 46

Beware The Six License Terms Of Death 48

Be Assertive But Reasonable 50

When To Be Extra Assertive 51

Pick Your Battles 51

Chapter 8 **Understanding Approval Plans** **53**

The Logic Of Approval Plans 53

How Do They Do It? .54

What Are Those Other Criteria? 54

Books In The Twilight Zone 55

Technical Processing And Bibliographic Records . .56

Approval Plan Discounts 57

III. Building And Maintaining The Library-Vendor Relationship

Chapter 9 **Putting Out Fires** **61**

Be Assertive But Reasonable 61

Being Assertive 62

Unacceptable Vendor Responses 62

Being Assertive With Scammers 63

Being Reasonable 64

Avoid Making Unreasonable Demands 64

Be Civil 66

Don't Assume Treachery When Human Error Is More
Likely 68

How To Tell When You Are Being Cheated 69

Chapter 10 **Preventing Fires** **71**

Put Your Best People On The Phone 71

Submitting Orders I: Boring Is Beautiful 73

Submitting Orders II: The Joy Of Autocracy 74

Know Who Your Friends Are 76

Watch Your E-Mail 77

Be Assertive But Reasonable 77

Chapter 11 **Working With Sales Representatives** **79**

Keep Your Appointments 80

On The Flipside 82

An Exception To The Punctuality Rule 83

Got Problems? Give Specifics 84

Let Her Sell 86

Let Your No Be No 86

Interacting With Sales Reps At Conferences 87

Be Assertive But Reasonable 89

Chapter 12 **Working With Customer Service Representatives 91**

You May Not Be Equals, But You Are Both Customers 91

Treat The Vendor As An "Internal Customer" 92

Make It Easy For The Vendor To Serve You Well . .93

Be Assertive But Reasonable 95

Let Mercy Temper Justice 97

Chapter 13 **Tracking Vendor Performance** **99**

Fulfillment Rates 99

Claim Responses 101

How Frequently Do You Have To Claim? 101

How Well Does The Vendor Respond To Claims? .102

Analyzing The Quality Of Customer Service 103

Analyzing Invoicing Practices 103

Analyzing Coverage 104

Technical Processing 105

IV. Ending (Or Avoiding) The Library-Vendor Relationship

Chapter 14   Switching Vendors **111**

Bad Reasons For Dropping A Vendor 111

Good Reasons For Changing Vendors 114

Managing The Switch 117

Leaving Your Bridges Intact 118

Chapter 15   Dealing With Unsolicited Materials **121**

What You Should Be Watching For 121

If You Did Not Order It, It Is Yours 123

What If The Vendor Did Talk To Someone In My
Library? 124

Standing Up For Yourself: A Model 125

Should You Ever Give In? 127

Chapter16   Working With Problem Vendors **129**

Defining The Problem Vendor 129

How Can You Avoid Them? 132

When You Must Deal With Problem Vendors 134

Chapter 17   Understanding The Ethics Of Vendor Relations .**139**

Your Ethical Duty To Your Patrons 140

Your Ethical Duty To Your Vendors 140

The ALCTS Statement Of Principles And Standards 141

Conclusion **149**

Appendices

A. Rules Of Thumb 151

B. Glossary 157

Index **167**

About the Author **169**

FOREWORD

In the past ten years, acquisitions and collection development departments and practices have changed dramatically. Gone are the days when ordering took place over the telephone and publishers' catalogs were lined up in alphabetical order for consultation.

Those old tried and true methods have been replaced instead by e-mail and the World Wide Web of ubiquitous information. Yet, librarians still attempt to order the best materials for their patrons in a timely manner at the best possible prices.

This how-to-do-it manual explores tried-and-true techniques of acquisitions librarianship as well as many of the innovations that make today's acquisitions work more multi-faceted. The relationship among publishers, librarians, and vendors is at the heart of the process. This manual explores topics like being a good customer, issuing a request for proposal, negotiating a license agreement, understanding approval plans, tracking vendor performance, working with problem vendors, dealing with unsolicited materials, and the ethics of vendor relations. Further reading lists allow you to delve deeper into areas that interest you.

I have shown this manual to my acquisitions order assistant who found it very valuable. This is a good basic introduction for new staff and/or others in the library field who need to know more about acquisitions. It could also a possibly serve as an introductory text for a technical services course in library school. My library will definitely order it when it comes out—several copies.

Katina Strauch
Head, Collection Development, College of Charleston Libraries
Editor, Against the Grain
strauchk@cofc.edu

PREFACE

Librarians and library support staff deal with library materials and service providers daily. Usually these interactions are harmonious; librarians, publishers and vendors recognize their synergistic relationship and the advantages of working well together. But, when problems occasionally arise, friction results. *Buying and Contracting for Resources and Services: A How-To-Do-It Manual for Librarians* serves two primary goals: to help you avoid these problems, if possible, and to help you quickly and professionally solve problems that do arise.

In library school you learned many good and valuable skills. But unless your experience was quite unusual, your course work did not teach you a set of strategies for working effectively with publishers, vendors and other library service providers. Yet many librarians devote significant time and energy to interacting with vendors. *Buying and Contracting for Resources and Services* is designed especially for people new to this area of running a library—recent graduates from library school, newly hired classified staff employees, or veteran workers who have recently moved from another professional niche into one that brings them into more regular contact with vendors and publishers. The guide can also serve as a resource for sales representatives and front-line staff employed by publishers, vendors, and service providers.

Though, as you will see, out of necessity I discuss the tasks associated with acquisition work, the bulk of the book centers on the "art" of doing business with vendors, publishers, and other service providers. You may think of vendor relations as a topic of interest only to acquisitions, serials, and collection development librarians. But reference librarians field sales calls on a regular basis, library directors are often directly involved with the selection and purchase of major capital items such as server networks and integrated library systems, and administrative staff regularly deal with supply companies, customer service representatives and salespersons. Many managing librarians, who may only occasionally interact directly with vendors, supervise others for whom such interactions are a matter of daily routine; these managers need to understand and know how to apply basic principles of effective relationship-building and relationship-maintenance with vendors in order to supervise their staffs.

ONE RECURRING THEME

You will notice a recurring theme in this book: "be assertive but reasonable." If the book had to be summarized in one phrase, that would be it. Assertiveness and reasonableness are two of the librarian's most powerful tools, and they are never more essential than when dealing with vendors. You must be assertive: you are disbursing what is, in many cases, a tremendous amount of money to your vendors, and that money is not yours. It is your duty as an employee of your institution (and, in many cases, of your state or city, as well) to be careful with its limited resources, which means insisting that in exchange for the amount paid out, vendors deliver their goods and services in good order. There is no place for tentativeness or diffidence when working with vendors.

On the other hand, you must also be reasonable: just as there is no place for tentativeness or diffidence in dealing with vendors, there is also no place for paranoia or vitriol. Except in rare cases (some of which will be dealt with specifically in later chapters of this book), your vendors are not trying to cheat you. Nor are they unconcerned with your needs or your institution's goals. Yes, they do want your money. But not only do most vendors understand that cheating and otherwise abusing their customers is a bad way to increase their share of the library market, they also are run, in the vast majority of cases, by genuinely honorable people, who wish to do the right thing and who work in the business that they do because they want to assist librarians in distributing information to their patrons. With a few exceptions, the world of scholarly publishing and library services does not attract heartless tycoons and bottom-line-driven greedheads. Unscrupulous companies and incompetent or malicious employees are certainly out there, but they are a distinct minority.

ORGANIZATION

Buying and Contracting for Resources and Services: A How-To-Do-It Manual for Librarians takes you through a logical progression of service and vendor-relations issues, beginning with basic matters of etiquette, and proceeding through the establishment and maintenance of a relationship with a vendor, before addressing the thorny problems that must be dealt with when terminating those relations. A final section discusses constructive ways of dealing with unethical and otherwise problematic vendors, and with ethical issues that you should consider when assessing your own policies and behavior. Throughout each part, examples and case studies will help you relate the basic principles under discussion to your own situation and experiences. The examples are mostly hypothetical, though some draw on elements of real-life situations on both sides of the library-vendor relationship. "Rules of Thumb" appear in the margins.

Note: In order to maintain gender balance without constantly shuffling male and female pronouns throughout the book, I refer to all librarians as "he" and all vendor representatives as "she." When referring to a vendor, publisher, or library as an organization, I refer to the entity as "it."

Part I, "Learning the Essentials of Vendor Relations," comprises chapters 1-3. This first section introduces the primary parties—vendors and customers—and introduces the rules of engagement that pertain to their relationship.

Chapter 1, "Working with Vendors: The State of the Art," offers an overview of the new world in which acquisitions, serials, and collection development librarians and library staff now work. E-mail and the World Wide Web have drastically changed the way library workers perform many of their duties, making some tasks quicker and easier and others more complicated and difficult, and creating whole new categories of work that did not previously exist. This chapter explains some of those changes, outlining some of those new tasks and warning the reader about potential pitfalls in the new landscape.

Chapter 2, "Being a Good Customer," puts to rest the idea that "the customer is always right," and discusses the importance of maintaining a balance between being demanding and being reasonable. There are some services you can and should demand from your vendors, and there are others that you should not expect vendors to do as a matter of course; examples of both are provided here. This chapter also addresses the strategic importance of simply being pleasant in your dealings with vendors, pointing out that a failure to do so will undermine not only the effectiveness of your communications with them, but also the professional esteem in which they hold you and your staff.

Chapter 3, "Getting Off on the Right Foot," goes a bit deeper than the previous chapter and discusses specific points of etiquette, which will help you keep things running smoothly in your dealings with publishers and vendors. It addresses such basic (but often overlooked) principles as the importance of identifying yourself fully by name and institution when calling a vendor, knowing the vendor's "lingo," returning telephone and e-mail messages promptly and professionally, and being appropriately assertive.

Part II explores "Establishing Successful Vendor Relations." In this section, we delve into issuing a request for proposals and actually creating new relationships with vendors, as well as following through with the fine points of negotiating terms.

Chapter 4, "Issuing a Request for Proposals," describes principles and strategies that can ease the often arduous process of issuing requests for proposals and fielding responses to them. Here I advise librarians to ask only for what they really want (and are prepared to handle), to give vendors adequate time to respond, and to allow room for negotiation of key points. Tips on being a good host and ways of helping ensure that the presentation goes smoothly are covered here as well, as is the importance of following up quickly and providing constructive feedback to the competing vendors.

Chapter 5, "Establishing a New Service," discusses the process of setting up a new service arrangement between a vendor and a library. Using the establishment of an approval plan as a model, this chapter covers such important behind-the-scenes issues as settling internal arguments before the vendor arrives, making sure that someone is in charge and can keep the meetings running on schedule, the importance of setting (and sticking to) an agenda, the necessity of building a shared vocabulary of services, and the value of early face-to-face interaction between library and vendor staff. It also offers a week-by-week checklist of tasks to be performed before the meeting takes place—tasks such as reserving meeting rooms, setting the meeting schedules, distributing those schedules to attendees, making parking arrangements for the vendor, and double-checking to make sure you can accommodate the vendor's technical needs.

Chapter 6, "Negotiating Terms of Service," addresses principles that should guide you in negotiating discounts, service fees and other terms of service. It explains why libraries usually get discounts when ordering books from a jobber, but pay service fees when using a subscription agent, and describes the factors that lead to larger or smaller discounts and fees. This chapter also discusses status reporting and cancellation policies, as well as some of the most common approaches to invoicing and returns.

Chapter 7, "Negotiating a License Agreement," discusses what is, for many librarians, one of the most challenging aspects of the modern information marketplace: the license agreement. It explains why it is essential that you pay attention to license terms, discusses the difference between binding contracts and non-binding "contracts of adhesion," outlines common license terms to which no library should ever agree, and offers some specific advice on the negotiation process.

Chapter 8, "Understanding Approval Plans," gives an overview of what has become one of the most common services used by academic (and many public) libraries: the approval plan. An approval plan allows the library to define categories of books that it is interested in adding to its collection; a vendor then sends books that fit those criteria, and the library may keep or return them as it sees fit. This allows librarians to spend less time researching and ordering books that are obvious choices for their collection, and more time using their expertise more productively. This chapter gives an overview of the way approval plans are set up and organized, the logic behind their operation, and some of the options that are typically available to library customers.

Chapter 9, "Putting Out Fires," discusses methods and strategies for solving the problems that will inevitably arise when libraries and vendors work together. It gives examples of unacceptable vendor responses to library concerns (and suggests ways of dealing with such responses), as well as examples of unreasonable expectations that librarians sometimes harbor. It also describes telltale signs of bad faith or duplicity that every librarian should watch for, while pointing out that human error is almost always a more likely explanation than intentional treachery when vendor problems arise.

Chapter 10, "Preventing Fires," outlines ways that libraries can organize their work to minimize the necessity of putting out fires before the ignite. While a library cannot entirely prevent vendor error (or even wholly to prevent errors of its own), it can do many things to minimize the possibility of errors. These include ensuring that your most professional employees act as primary contacts with your vendors, submitting orders and claims both clearly and consistently, knowing how your vendors' internal departments are organized, who your contacts are, and monitoring your e-mail on a regular and consistent basis.

Chapter 11, "Working With Sales Representatives," offers pointers for keeping your relationships with sales reps both pleasant and productive. It discusses some basic principles of business etiquette, provides advice for dealing with the sales rep who is too aggressive or otherwise inappropriate in her approach, offers tips on making your complaints to sales reps specific and constructive, and touches on some of the particular issues that arise when interacting with sales reps at meetings or conferences.

Chapter 12, "Working With Customer Service Representatives," examines the concept of "internal" and "external" customers, and makes a case for treating your vendor's customer service reps as if they are internal customers—people within your organization who need to get consistent and accurate outputs from you and your staff in order to serve you well. Because most of your daily interactions with vendors will be mediated by customer service reps, it is important that you and your staff know how to make it easy for them to serve you well; this also means that you should insist on a high level of competence and professionalism on the rep's part.

Chapter 13, "Tracking Vendor Performance," outlines the three basic parameters of vendor fulfillment (timeliness, accuracy, and completeness) and different ways of tracking and analyzing the quality of their services. It considers approaches to analyzing a vendor's responsiveness to claims, the importance of keeping a history of vendor problems and the ways in which they were resolved, and criteria for judging the quality of a vendor's invoicing practices and technical processing.

Part IV discusses "Ending (or Avoiding) the Library-Vendor Relationship." These final four chapters take up the difficult side of dealing with vendors: switching vendors, eliminating unwanted solicitation, coping with problem vendors, and looking at the ethical issues inherent in the vendor-library relationship.

Chapter 14, "Switching Vendors," addresses the sensitive question of when it is appropriate to cease doing business with one vendor in favor of another. This chapter is organized into two sections: the first discusses insufficient reasons for dropping a vendor (problems that are only occasional, or are simply a part of doing business in the information industry, or that are actually your library's fault), and the second discusses problems that *should* lead you seriously to consider switching to another vendor (criminal or unethical behavior, chronic problems that the vendor is unable or unwilling to fix, ongoing unresponsiveness, fiscal trouble or mismanagement).

Chapter 15, "Dealing with Unsolicited Materials," examines your rights and responsibilities dealing with vendors that send you books, journals or other materials that you have not ordered and then ask for payment. It cites and explains the relevant section of the U.S. Code, describes the different forms that these scamming maneuvers may take, and even offers a form letter you can use to respond to them. Other chapters in this book emphasize the importance of being reasonable and pleasant in dealing with vendors; this one advises that you be firm and immovable in resisting unscrupulous vendors' attempts to trick or coerce you into buying things you do not want.

Chapter 16, "Working With Problem Vendors," offers advice for those times when you have no choice but to deal with a vendor that is not necessarily dishonest or corrupt, but that is still difficult to do business with—whether because its products or services are inferior, the company is poorly managed, it is financially unstable, or it is technologically weak. This chapter offers examples of problem vendors and techniques for avoiding them where possible; where avoiding them is not possible, it suggests ways of making it clear to such vendors what their weaknesses are and what they can do to help compensate for them.

Chapter 17, "The Ethics of Vendor Relations," is primarily an examination of the *Statement of Principles and Standards of Acquisitions Practice* adopted in 1994 by the Association for Library Collections and Technical Services and ways in which it can be applied to everyday library practice.

Many chapters include references to articles for further reading. The Rules of Thumb you see scattered throughout the text are gathered into a separate appendix at the end of the book (Appendix A). I hope you will use this compilation as a summary or "quick guide" to material elucidated more fully in the book. I trust these ideas, observations, and suggestions will serve as a useful introduction, overview and reference resource for library staff in many different areas, but particularly those working in acquisitions, serials, and collection development.

ACKNOWLEDGMENTS

I gratefully acknowledge the support of my colleagues and staff at the University of Nevada, Reno Libraries, especially Steven D. Zink and Donnelyn Curtis. I am also grateful for the generous and indispensable input of a number of members of the vendor world, many of whom I count as close and valued friends and who, for obvious reasons, must remain anonymous. Thanks to my editor Michael Kelley at Neal-Schuman, who has been unfailingly patient and pleasant throughout the writing process. Portions of several chapters of this book originally appeared in shorter form as "How to Make Your Book Vendor Love You," in the April, 1998 issue of *Against the Grain*; I am grateful to editor Katina Strauch for allowing me to reuse them here.

I. LEARNING THE ESSENTIALS OF VENDOR RELATIONS

1

WORKING
WITH VENDORS:
THE STATE OF THE ART

Ask any librarian who has been working in acquisitions, serials, or collection development, for more than a decade or two, and he will tell you that almost everything about that work has changed drastically since the advent of the Internet in general and, in particular, of the World Wide Web. The Internet revolution has affected every task you perform and pertains to every topic we discuss in this book. Therefore, it might be a good idea to look at the general effects of that revolution on the relationship between libraries and vendors before turning to a closer examination of those specifics tasks and topics.

1.1   IT IS THE BEST OF TIMES, IT IS THE WORST OF TIMES

If you are new to the library profession, you can consider yourself lucky in many significant ways. For one thing, it has never been easier to communicate quickly and effectively with the vendors and publishers with whom you work. Until not very long ago, your day-to-day communications could take place only by mail (postal mail, that is) or telephone. You learned about upcoming publications either from printed announcements or from conversations with sales reps. Your only sources for publisher contact information were printed directories, most of which were out of date before they even reached your library. There was no such thing as an online discussion group, in which you could ask advice and discuss common problems with your colleagues.

The revolutionary changes that have taken place in the information world over the last fifteen years have brought tremendous relief in these areas. E-mail makes it possible not just to have conversations, but also to send and receive documents across huge distances almost instantaneously. Most publishers now maintain web sites that offer contact information, full online catalogs, and descriptions of upcoming books, all available at the click of a mouse. Online discussion groups have proliferated to the point that there is one (sometimes more than one) designed for workers in almost every area of the library. Online discussions allow you to tap the knowledge and experience of colleagues from around the world, and can often bring answers to knotty questions literally within minutes.

But as exciting as they are, these changes have, inevitably, introduced new problems of their own. E-mail traffic can be overwhelming—sore ears from long telephone conversations have, in many cases, been replaced by carpal tunnel syndrome brought on by extended periods of non-stop typing—and the ease of e-mail sometimes leads not to better communication, but merely to more of it. The proliferation of online discussion groups has sometimes had a similar effect on professional conversations, as participants get bogged down in long, argumentative exchanges or waste each other's time with unnecessary "me, too!" postings. The fact that you can receive product announcements electronically is a mixed blessing, depending on how relevant and numerous are the announcements you receive. Of course, the web sites of some publishers and vendors offer more frustration than enlightenment (though even the worst usually manage to be an improvement over what was available before the Internet).

Overall, though, it is probably fair to say that while the Internet has not made our lives any less busy, it has made the performance of many library tasks easier and more efficient. We still work full days, but most of us are able to accomplish quite a bit more and can do so with less stress and frustration.

But perhaps more significant than the changes the Internet has caused in the way we do existing tasks are the new library tasks that have appeared since its emergence. Many of these have a direct bearing on your work with vendors and publishers.

1.2 NEW LIBRARY TASKS FOR THE ONLINE WORLD

Working in an online environment requires skills and abilities both new and old, and sometimes what is needed is a combination of the two. For example, while e-mail messages have largely replaced letters as the most common form of business correspondence between libraries and vendors, the ability to write a good letter does not necessarily translate into the ability to write an effective e-mail message (or vice versa); so, both skills are necessary for a librarian who must work with vendors and publishers. But many of the tasks that our new information world requires us to perform are entirely new, and "native" to that new world. Among them are the following:

Setting up online access. Scholarly journal publication is moving with increasing swiftness from the print to the online realm. Reference

---

E-MAIL PLUSES

- It is much faster than "snail mail."
- It allows you to attach other documents.
- It allows you to embed links to other documents.
- It enables almost instantaneous virtual conversation.
- It makes it easy to archive messages you have sent.
- It allows you to file correspondence in your computer.
- It allows you to search the content of old correspondence.

E-MAIL MINUSES

- Since e-mail is fast and easy, you will get lots of it.
- Many of the messages you get will be ads or chain letters (junk e-mail).
- Because e-mail is a casual medium, messages are often sloppy and unclear.
- More e-mail means more typing, and more stress on hands and tendons.
- It is all too easy to send a message to the wrong person .

resources are doing the same. An online reference database, even one that is difficult to use, offers tremendous benefits (remote access, 24-hour availability, real-time updates, texts that are fully searchable, etc.) that its print counterpart cannot. Libraries and their patrons are increasingly turning away from print research materials and toward online resources. This means that acquisitions and serials departments—while still performing their traditional duties of ordering and invoice processing—are also being given the job of figuring out how to establish and maintain access to those online resources. This process involves a number of steps, including:

- Locating the correct URL for the online product, and distributing that URL to those in the library who will need to create links to it in the library catalog and web pages
- Negotiating license agreements (see Chapter 7)
- Determining and reporting the host institution's headcount and/or FTE enrollment
- Ensuring that both the vendor staff and the library staff know who should be contacted in the event of technical problems
- Ensuring that access is in place at the beginning of the license period

Online troubleshooting. One of the nice things about print materials is that once they are acquired, processed and shelved, they do not need much in the way of ongoing maintenance. They may fall apart occasionally, but when they do it is usually because of heavy use, which is easy enough to monitor during the circulation process. The same is not true of online products, which can become unavailable without warning and for no apparent reason. Worse, when a patron is frustrated in his attempts to access a database or retrieve a journal article, he may simply move on to another source without telling anyone about the problem, thus allowing the problem to persist indefinitely, until someone finally brings it to the library's attention. The more online resources you provide to your patrons, the less possible it becomes to monitor all of them on an ongoing basis. Catching and resolving online access problems is one of the newest and most time-consuming duties of twenty-first century acquisitions and serials departments.

Learning how to use vendor databases. The major book jobbers and subscription agents all have online databases that can be used, in various degrees and with varying levels of ease, to manage orders and to monitor account activity. Acquisitions and serials staff need to learn

---

A NEW SKILLSET FOR A NEW MILLENNIUM:

- Setting up online access
- Online troubleshooting
- Learning to use multiple online databases
- Finding, downloading and manipulating usage statistics
- Using search engines to find bibliographic data and publisher information
- Using e-mail appropriately

how to use these databases and will often need to train others (such as subject specialists who may use them to request desired titles) in their use, as well. Librarians in the acquisitions and serials areas will also need to determine, in consultation with their local system officers, whether and to what extent a vendor's database can interact with the library's local computer system, and whether that interaction can simplify or speed up the ordering and receiving of books and journals.

Finding, downloading, and manipulating usage statistics. Online journal packages and reference databases are often very expensive, and you will want to know whether the use they are getting is sufficient to justify the price your library is paying for them. An increasing number of online service providers offer usage statistics for their products, though the quality and depth of the data offered varies significantly from vendor to vendor. Every library needs someone (usually from the ranks of the acquisitions, serials, or collection development staff) who, before the product is purchased, can first of all make a determination as to whether the statistics offered by the vendor are sufficient, and second of all take charge of retrieving, manipulating, and interpreting those statistics. This can be a daunting and time-consuming task, and it is one that draws on skills that were not really necessary to acquisitions work only a few years ago.

Using search engines to find bibliographic data and publisher information. When the primary sources for publisher information and bibliographic data were printed directories like *Literary Marketplace* and *Books in Print*, gathering such information was a relatively simple and straightforward (if unreliable) proposition: there were only a few ways to look up a book or publisher in those sources, those approaches were easily mastered, and if what you wanted was not there, you could see very quickly that it was not there. With the advent of the World Wide Web, much more information is available and finding it can be much more complicated. As the Web grows and as increasing numbers of publishers and vendors figure out how to establish a Web presence, more and more of the information you need is going online and becoming freely available to you at the touch of a mouse-button—assuming that you can find the desired web site. Online search engines such as Google (http://www.google.com) and AltaVista (http://www.altavista.com) will help you zero in on the sites you need, as long as you know how to use them. Google is exceptionally powerful, but it relies mainly on a strategy of multiple keywords to narrow your search results; AltaVista allows you to formulate more specific searches, but does not index as many web sites. Users can employ many other search engines on the Web, of course, all with different strengths and weaknesses, some with industry-specific strengths. Trial and error (and regularly consulting the search engines' "Searching Tips" pages) will lead you to the strategies that work best for you.

Using e-mail appropriately. E-mail is one of the most powerful productivity tools of the new century. Cheaper than the telephone and potentially almost as fast, e-mail also makes it easy to keep an accurate record of one's interactions with a vendor and to retrace your steps when something goes wrong. Inevitably, and unfortunately, e-mail has its downsides as well. Because e-mail messages are usually less formal than business letters, it is easy to let e-mail messages lapse from efficient casualness into unprofessional sloppiness. And because e-mail makes it so easy to distribute messages to many people at once, a lapse in vigilance can result in messages being sent to the wrong people. Sloppy writing may, but does not usually, carry serious professional consequences—accidentally sending the wrong e-mail to the wrong person, however, can be disastrous. Consider the experience of one customer service rep, who had just had a very frustrating e-mail exchange with a librarian who, he felt, was being unreasonable in her demands and inappropriate in her approach. The rep forwarded a copy of one of the librarian's more obnoxious messages to the sales rep who had responsibility for that library, adding a note that said, basically, "Look what I've had to put up with today." The sales rep responded with a sympathetic note, agreeing with the customer service rep that the librarian in question was obviously out of line. Unfortunately, when he sent his note back to the customer service rep, he accidentally hit "reply to all" instead of "reply"—and the librarian got a copy of the message as well. Library staff need to learn not only how to use e-mail systems, but also how to compose professional e-mail messages and distribute them appropriately.

> **Rule of Thumb:** *Use e-mail rather than the telephone as often as you can, and if possible, set your e-mail system to automatically archive messages that you send. A searchable archive of your sent messages can be a lifesaver.*

1.3 IT'S STILL THE WILD, WILD WEB

The World Wide Web has developed quickly, and its robust development continues unabated. Standards and "best practices" for web site design are still being established; the legal environment for the Internet is still being fiercely debated. Librarians know and openly discuss the fact that they are often confused about how to deal with the Web and how best to harness it for their patrons. Because publishers have market positions to defend and (often) shareholders to keep happy, they are usually less willing to discuss their own misgivings in public. But do not be fooled—most publishers are under just as much pressure as librarians to get content online, and are just as befuddled about how to do it in a way that fits the business model and shareholder expectations of the publisher.

On the one hand, librarians need to be patient with publishers and vendors and realize that this is a difficult and confusing time for them as well as for us. Do not assume that just because a vendor or publisher makes confident noises in public about its Web presence, it really knows what it is doing. On the other hand, we need to be careful that we get value for our money, and we need to hold our vendors to appropriate standards of service. (We will discuss specific ways of doing so throughout this book.) We should also bear in mind that being active in the information world during a period of intense and fundamental change puts us in a position to help shape that change. If we are smart, we will look for opportunities to help publishers design their products and pricing structures to achieve a win-win outcome.

FURTHER READING:

Latham, Joyce. "The World Online: IT Skills for the Practical Professional." *American Libraries* 31 (March 2000), 40.

Hock, Randolph. *The Extreme Searcher's Guide to Web Search Engines: A Handbook for the Serious Searcher.* 2nd ed. Medford, NJ: Information Today, 2001.

2 BEING A GOOD CUSTOMER

2.1 THE CUSTOMER IS NOT ALWAYS RIGHT

If you want to deal effectively and professionally with your vendors, put out of your mind the idea that you, the customer, are always right. Your vendors may act as if you are, because treating the customer that way is generally a good idea; it produces sales and retains customers. But do not be fooled. Persisting in the illusion that you are always right will only impede the ability of you and your staff to develop the skills and practices that you need to make your department function smoothly, to work effectively with vendors and, ultimately, to serve your patrons well.

Of course, we all understand this. No librarian really believes that every problem that arises in the course of his dealings with publishers and vendors is the other side's fault. Furthermore, we sometimes decide not to worry too much about who is at fault; sometimes it makes sense simply to solve the problem and get on with life.

But in some situations it is vitally important to figure out who is at fault—not so that you can assign blame, but because the problem is one that you will not be able to prevent in the future unless you know how it arose. In these cases, your greatest asset will be your ability to look dispassionately at your established processes, at the chain of events that led to this particular error or problem, and at the skills and limitations of your staff (as well as your own), and to take or assign responsibility according to the facts. Even in these situations, though, you should take care not to dwell unnecessarily on questions of blame, but to focus on solutions and future prevention.

2.2 HOW TO BE A SQUEAKY WHEEL

Finding a balance between being appropriately demanding and strategically pleasant can be difficult, and in some situations your approach will have to tilt a bit more in one of those directions than the other. When trying to get a vendor to do something—change your shipping schedule, deepen your discount, accept a return, reinstate access despite a late renewal invoice—your approach should be determined by asking yourself the following question:

AM I INSISTING ON SOMETHING THE VENDOR OWES ME, OR AM I ASKING FOR A FAVOR?

If your answer is the former, then the balance of your approach should tilt toward the "squeaky wheel" side, whereas if you are asking the vendor to make an exception for you or provide a special service, your approach should be more gentle. This may seem obvious, but it is not as obvious to some as it should be. Of course, some requests do not fall clearly into one or the other category. Here is a list of some potential requests that a library might make of a vendor, with a possible breakdown into categories:

Things you can demand:	Something that falls somewhere in between:	Things you can ask for:
Professional service Timely delivery Carefully packed and professionally shipped materials Accurate fulfillment of orders The right to return a product that was sent in error	Discount enhancement in the wake of increased business	A specific day of shipment Customized shelf-ready processing Discount enhancement A specific customer service or sales representative Access extension when payment is delayed

If what you are doing is asking the vendor for a favor, make sure your vendor can tell that you understand you are asking for a favor. If your request comes across as a demand, your contact person will be sorely tempted (and well within her rights) to deny the request—if for no other reason than simply to make it clear that she does have the option to say no when you make an unreasonable demand. Consider the exchange below:

> **Librarian:** I need you to authorize the return of a book that we got from you last week.
>
> **Vendor:** OK. Have you done any physical processing on the book?
>
> **Librarian:** We ordered it shelf-ready.
>
> **Vendor:** Oh, well, that's going to be a problem; we can't accept returns on shelf-ready books unless there is an error of some kind on our part. Did we send you the wrong book, or did we mess up the processing in some way?
>
> **Librarian:** No, it's just that we received another copy as a gift after we sent you our order, and the gift copy has been processed. We don't need a second copy.
>
> **Vendor:** I can understand that, but I can't authorize the return unless there was some error on our part. That was part of our agreement when we first set up shelf-ready services with your library.

In the example above, the librarian approached the situation as if he had the right to demand approval for his return, which of course he did not. If the vendor had approved the return, it would have set a dangerous precedent; the rep did exactly the right thing by saying no.

On the other hand, consider this exchange:

> **Librarian:** I need to ask a favor of you. We ordered a shelf-ready book from you a few weeks ago, and it arrived today. The problem is that we were given another copy of the book as a gift after we sent the order, and we forgot to contact you and cancel it. I know this was our fault, but is there any way we could return it? The processing is minimal—just a security tape and a property stamp.
>
> **Vendor:** I wish I could, but even that minimal level of processing makes the book impossible for us to re-sell. But maybe there's something else we can do to help you out.

> *Rule of Thumb:* Do not do things that will make your vendor want to say "no."

Note, in the second case above, that the librarian still was not given clearance to return the processed book. But by handling the request in an appropriate way, he left the vendor rep trying to figure out a way to help instead of feeling the need to remind him of the rules to which he had previously agreed.

2.3 IF YOU ACT LIKE A JERK, YOU WILL LOOK INCOMPETENT

All of us have dealt with difficult people: people who do not really know what they are doing and try to cover up for it with bluster and impatience; or, people who are rude, not so much because they mean to be, but because they simply do not seem interested in whether they are providing decent service; or, people who obviously hate their jobs and are just trying to get through the day with as little irritation and inconvenience as possible, so that they can get out of there and go home. Think about the interactions you have had with people like this. Ask yourself how you would rate those people for competence on a scale of one to ten.

Now think of someone else you have interacted with in a professional setting, but this time make it someone who was pleasant and seemed interested in making sure your needs were met. Maybe it was a cashier at the grocery story who noticed that your bag of flour was open and quickly dispatched someone to get you another one while he finished ringing up your other groceries; maybe it was a clerk at the Division of Motor Vehicles who, contrary to your every expectation, fixed a problem for you quickly and professionally while you waited, instead of sending you away to fix it yourself. When you think of people like this and imagine how their minds work, do you assume that they approach their duties sloppily? Do you suspect that they know their jobs thoroughly? In short, which group of people seems the most competent to you—those who have dealt with you in a rude or aggressive way, or those who have been thoughtful and aware of your needs?

The lesson here is that if you are nice, people are most likely to assume that you are competent.

Is this fair? Not really. The correlation of niceness to competence is by no means perfect, and some of the smartest and most skillful people you will ever work with may be personally unpleasant; conversely, the sweetest person in the world may also be professionally hopeless. It is worth pointing out, again, that firmness is part of professional niceness. But aggressive rudeness will generally mark you as someone who is at least socially inept and, perhaps, professionally incompetent, as well.

One last point: obviously, when you are dealing with a vendor it is primarily the vendor's job to be nice to you, not vice-versa. But we are not talking about whose job it is to be nice—we are talking about how you can present yourself as a competent and reliable professional. Do not undermine that presentation with personal behavior that misrepresents your abilities.

> **Rule of Thumb:** If you are nice, people are more likely to assume that you are competent.

3 GETTING OFF ON THE RIGHT FOOT

3.1 SAY YOUR NAME

Every one of us has had painful experiences like the following: The phone rings. You pick it up and say hello, and the caller simply starts talking, assuming that you will recognize his or her voice immediately. The voice is familiar, of course, but that does not mean you can put a face to it, so you carry on the conversation in an agony of head-scratching and noncommittal responses, hoping against hope that you will figure out who this person is before you are forced to confess your confusion.

Such situations are difficult enough when they involve friends or (even worse) family. But when they involve professional relationships the stress is amplified. For a vendor, few things are more nerve-wracking than having a customer on the phone—especially an upset customer—and trying to respond to his concerns intelligently while simultaneously figuring out who the caller is, what institution he represents, and the nature of the problem that he is describing.

Because we are the vendors' customers, we do not have to worry too much about this ourselves. If a vendor rep calls and fails to identify herself, we can simply inquire, "I'm sorry, would you tell me who you are and why you're calling?" without too much fear of embarrassment. But on the vendor side, things are a bit more delicate. Consider this conversation, which is based on a real-life experience:

> **Caller:** Hi, this is Dave from Johnson Library. I need to ask some questions about our approval plan.
>
> **Vendor Rep** (who has no fewer than six Daves in her contacts list and who has never heard of Johnson Library, but realizes that this must be an approval customer): Sure, Dave, how can I help you?
>
> **Caller:** Well, there's a book that I just saw in the campus bookstore yesterday, and it seems like it would fit our profile but we haven't received it on approval yet. Could you check and see whether it's on the way?
>
> **Vendor Rep** (who can now deduce that this person is calling from an academic library and is racking her brain for customers in her group that work in a Johnson Library, which is obviously on the campus of some academic institution): I'm sure I can figure that

out for you. Do you have the ISBN?

Caller: Yes, it's 0975288621.

Vendor Rep (looking up the approval-plan history for this book and seeing that it was sent to 42 libraries): Let's see, Dave, it does look like we've handled it on approval fairly recently. (Suddenly, the rep is inspired!) Can you tell me which of your approval plans you expected to see it on?

Caller (sounding puzzled): Our Humanities plan, of course.

Vendor Rep (trying to recover): Well, right, Humanities obviously. But do you remember the plan number?

Caller: I think it's number 277.

Vendor Rep (with enormous relief): That's right, 277. Yes, this book is on the way to you; it was invoiced and shipped out two days ago.

If Dave from Johnson Library had simply borne in mind some basic principles of phone etiquette, two things about this conversation would have been different. First, the conversation would have been more brief, which would have been good for him; second, the vendor rep would have run significantly less risk of a heart attack. Both of these are desirable outcomes. To achieve them, always offer both your full name and the name of your institution when you call your vendor. If you are calling from an academic library, bear in mind that to most of your vendors, the name of your institution is the name of the college or university for which you work—not the name of the library itself. For example, then, Dave from Johnson Library should have introduced himself this way: "Hi, this is Dave Bishop from the library at the University of Eastern Montana." Then the vendor rep could have responded with "Of course, Dave, how nice to hear from you again. Getting much snow this year? No? Well, what can I help you with today?"

Save yourself and your vendors some embarrassment by always offering the following whenever you call:

- Your name (first and last)
- The full name of your institution (if you are in an academic library, that means the name of the host college or university, not the name of the library itself)

3.2   KNOW THE LINGO

Every organization has a more or less unique internal language. It consists of acronyms, shorthand references, locally-grown slang terms and terms for local practices that are immediately understood throughout the organization, but probably sound like nonsense to anyone from the outside. These in-group languages are very valuable—they make it easy to conduct internal business quickly and efficiently, and they can also foster a sense of group cohesion. However, they can get in the way when doing business with people from outside the organization, if employees are not careful about how they use local lingo around those who do not understand it.

Happily married couples will tell you that a good marriage comes not from each partner contributing fifty percent, but from each contributing what seems like seventy-five or eighty percent. The same can be said of good customer-vendor relations, especially where building a shared vocabulary is concerned. As a customer, you should expect your vendor to have a general grasp of some of your local language—the names of your branch libraries, the acronyms you use to refer to your local system and its components, and what you mean by terms like "claim" and "serial." On the flip side, as a customer, you will do both yourself and your vendor a big favor by being as conversant as possible with the vendor's lingo. You have many vendors to deal with, of course, and your vendor serves many libraries, so neither of you can be expected to understand the other's every arcane term and acronym. But some effort to learn the local language will reap dividends for both of you.

Be especially cautious when using terms that have ambiguous meanings. You may not be aware that some of the terms you use commonly (and without any confusion) in your institution may be used differently by others within the profession and in the vendor world. Some of these terms will be considered in detail in Chapter 5; they include:

- Account
- Claim
- Status
- Management Report
- Firm Order
- Profile
- Series/Serial/Continuation
- Subscription

Taking care of these two tasks early in the relationship, and updating that knowledge frequently, will greatly minimize confusion and error for both you and your vendors.

> **Rule of Thumb:** *Every minute you spend learning your vendor's jargon will result in five minutes saved in your subsequent dealings with that vendor.*

> Acquiring a common language consists of two main efforts:
>
> - Learning each other's unique terms
> - Learning each other's assigned meanings for common but ambiguous terms

3.3   THE HEARTBREAK OF JARGON

The poorly considered use of professional jargon with those outside the profession (or in different areas of it) can lead to problems both minor and colossal. Consider the amusing, yet slightly hair-raising, experience of one library administrator, as he and his colleagues met with architects to make preliminary plans for the layout of a new library building:

> We were discussing the layout of the new library's main floor, where we were hoping to integrate some service points that, in our current building, were a bit too widely dispersed. At one point we had to figure out where to put the elevator shaft, and we found what seemed like a good location near the rear of the building. At this point one of the architects said, "And of course, we'll put Circulation behind the elevator shaft." All the library staff looked at the architects in bewilderment. "Put Circulation behind the elevator shaft? Are you crazy?" Now the architects looked bewildered. "Of course," they said. "How could you not have Circulation behind the elevator shaft? Unless it's going to be embedded in the rear wall you really have no choice." Now everyone was confused and starting to get just a bit distressed. Each side of this discussion thought the other one had gone completely insane. Eventually, we figured out that, in architectural jargon, "circulation" means "room for people to walk," and the fog finally lifted. We were hearing the word "Circulation" with a capital C, meaning the department, whereas the architects meant "circulation" with a small c, meaning space for people to circulate. We all laughed, but it was sobering to realize how quickly communication can break down when you don't share the same understanding of terms.

In this case, the term "circulation" was professional jargon on both sides of the discussion, and the term had completely different meanings for the two parties. To avoid this sort of misunderstanding between you and your vendors, you and your staff should be careful not to assume that terms you take for granted are understood in the same way by those you deal with outside of your institution.

3.4 ASSUME GOOD FAITH

When dealing with a vendor, especially when problems arise, it is very important that you bear in mind one simple fact: it is highly unlikely that the vendor is actually trying to cheat you. This is not an ironclad rule, of course—there are unethical vendors in the marketplace, and you are likely to run into a few of them in the course of your career.

But, they are an exception. Especially if you are dealing with an established vendor with whom you have a long relationship, it will almost always be more accurate (and constructive) to assume that problems are most likely caused by human or mechanical error, and that they arise unintentionally, than to react in a defensive or accusatory way.

In Chapter 15, we will discuss ways of dealing with vendors that are genuinely dishonest and predatory. The problems that such vendors pose are serious and you should not underestimate them. But established vendors with whom you deal on a regular basis generally have much more to lose from trying to cheat you than they do from dealing with you honestly and professionally. That said, it is important to hold your vendors to a high standard of service and honesty. If you have a clear reason to suspect your vendor of inappropriate practices or dishonest behavior, do not hesitate to bring it up with your rep. But you should probably not consider most garden-variety errors—books missing from shipments, serial titles that are late in arriving—to be clear evidence of treachery. Start with the assumption that your vendor is honest and dealing in good faith, and proceed from that point.

3.5 RETURN MESSAGES PROMPTLY AND PROFESSIONALLY

You should expect your vendors to return your phone calls and respond to your e-mail messages within twenty-four hours, especially if you are reporting a problem. A good vendor rep will do so even if she has not yet solved the problem or found the answer to your question. A quick call or message that says, "I'm still working on the problem" lets you know that your needs have not been forgotten. Similarly, you should do your best to respond promptly to calls and e-mail messages from your vendors. In part, this is simple courtesy, but it also makes it easier for your vendors to serve you well.

When making or returning phone calls or responding to e-mail messages, take a moment to be sure that they are formulated professionally. When leaving a voicemail message, speak clearly and a bit more slowly than you would in normal conversation. If you are leaving your phone number, say the numbers slowly and repeat them again at the end of your message, so that the person who is listening to the message has time to write them down. Double-check your e-mail messages for spelling and grammar errors before sending them. You want to avoid such errors in part to maintain a professional image, but also to avoid confusion. Grammatical errors sometimes make the meaning of your message unclear, and it will be embarrassing for both

Rule of Thumb: *Respond to all vendors' voicemail and e-mail messages within twenty-four hours, even if you do not yet have a complete answer to the vendor's question.*

Rule of Thumb: *Never hit <send> until you have reread your e-mail message at least one time through and double-checked the "To" field.*

of you if your vendor rep has to write back, asking that you explain yourself more clearly.

3.6 BE ASSERTIVE BUT REASONABLE

This is a principle to which we will return repeatedly during this book. As a customer, it is essential that you maintain a balance between being assertive and being reasonable. Too little assertiveness, and you will send the message that your vendor's business is safe with you regardless of whether the vendor is serving you well. You will also send the message that you are not on top of things and that the vendor can probably let quality slide without fear of you or your staff noticing. On the other hand, if you are unreasonable in your demands, at least two things will happen: First, you will be chronically disappointed by your vendor's inability to live up to your unreasonable expectations. Second, your vendor will likely start looking for ways to say "no" to you, just to keep you aware of the fact that you cannot have everything. You do not want to be in this position. Yes, it is your vendor's job to make you happy, not vice versa. But if you make your vendor miserable, you will end up regretting it. Your goal should be to cultivate both a reputation for sharpness, competence and precision in your dealings with your vendor, and a reputation for fair-mindedness and a willingness to compromise where necessary.

FURTHER READING:

Shu-Hsien Lai Chen, Shu-Hsien Lai. "Etiquette in E-mail Communication." *Journal of Educational Media & Library Sciences* (June 2001), 347.

Sturges, Paul. "Remember the Human: the First Rule of Netiquette, Librarians and the Internet." *Online Information Review* 26 (2002), 209.

II. ESTABLISHING SUCCESSFUL VENDOR RELATIONS

4 ISSUING A REQUEST FOR PROPOSALS

There are certain terms and phrases that, when spoken, are guaranteed to produce an involuntary shudder in even the most stouthearted librarian. One of those is "RFP," which stands for Request for Proposals. An RFP is a document that you send out to vendors whom you wish to consider as service providers. It explains all the details relevant to your service needs: what services you are interested in, how much you are willing to pay for them, what criteria you will use in judging vendor proposals, when you plan to make your decision, when you expect to initiate the new service or services. Usually, you will request written responses to your RFP, and will then ask vendors who seem like the best fit for your needs to come and make a presentation at your library.

Many libraries are governed by state laws or other rules that require them to issue an RFP whenever they are going to make a very large capital purchase or enter into a major service agreement with a vendor. Even in situations where an RFP is not required, it may well be worth the effort to issue one. A quick search of the library literature will lead you to many articles and several books that address the RFP process in detail; a few are listed at the end of this chapter. Here we will discuss some general principles that will help you to plan and carry out your RFPs with the least possible amount of grief and inconvenience—to both you and your vendors.

4.1 BE CAREFUL WHAT YOU WISH FOR

When you issue an RFP, it should include a detailed list of the services you will expect from the vendor you eventually select. Make sure that your list of requirements is realistic. By all means, solicit the input of all affected library staff, but once you have compiled your wish list, take the time to examine it with a critical eye. Ask yourself questions like these:

Are we ready to implement all of the services we have listed as "required?" Obviously, it would be foolish to require your vendor to provide a service that your library is not yet ready to handle (or is not making active preparations to be able to handle). But the mere fact

Two questions to ask your-self about your RFP:

• Are we ready to imple-ment all the services we have listed as "required?"
• Can our requirements be ranked in importance?

Rule of Thumb: If your RFP calls on vendors to do the impossible, then only liars will respond.

Before the presentation:

• Only invite serious candi-dates.
• Allow some flexibility in time and format.
• Notify all key staff and encourage them to attend.
• Make sure you have ade-quate technical support on hand.

After the presentation:

• Notify all contending ven-dors promptly.
• Provide feedback to all participants.

that it would obviously be foolish may not be enough to dissuade someone on your library staff from lobbying for just such a require-ment. Resist the temptation simply to create a list of requirements based on the "wouldn't it be nice if…" criterion. If you have no plans to implement, say, online ordering or electronic invoicing, there is no point in insisting that vendors responding to the RFP be able to pro-vide those services.

Can our requirements be ranked in importance? If your RFP indicates (whether intentionally or not) that all listed requirements are equally important, then you will run the risk of discouraging the ven-dor that might have been your best overall choice, but cannot supply one or two of the services for which you actually have the least press-ing need. While weeding out inappropriate vendors is one important function of the RFP process, you want to be careful not to weed out the one that may turn out to be the best fit for your needs.

4.2 GIVE THEM TIME AND LET THEM NEGOTIATE

Do not put the vendors to whom you send your RFP in the position of having to rush their responses. Give them enough time to answer com-pletely and carefully. In general, you should plan to leave at least one month between the date that you issue your RFP and the due date for responses. Sixty days is even better. Remember that the vendors may need to contact you during that time in order to clarify something in your RFP, or to ask for additional information.

You should also make it clear in your RFP which terms and service criteria you are willing to negotiate, and which ones are nonnegotiable. When in doubt about a particular term or criterion, make it negotiable. Remember that on certain points, especially discount, vendors will give you a quote in response to the RFP if required to do so, but that they may well be willing to make adjustments based on face-to-face negoti-ation, if they are not tossed out of the running early on. Of course, if a vendor's response on a particular point strikes you as odd or unreason-able, take the time to make a phone call yourself if the point in question is liable to remove an otherwise desirable vendor from serious consid-eration. The vendor may be more flexible on that point than is immedi-ately obvious from its response to the RFP.

4.3   BE A GOOD HOST

When the responses have been analyzed and the vendor pool cut down to a workable size, you will select several vendors—probably no more than three—to come and give presentations in person. Planning and hosting these presentations can be stressful for all involved. However, if you take a few simple precautions and apply several basic principles, you will find that you can significantly reduce everyone's stress load. (For some general planning principles that can be applied when organizing any large-scale vendor visit, see the Pre-Visit Checklist outlined in the next chapter.)

Only invite serious candidates. Do not invite a vendor out of politeness or concern for someone's feelings. Bear in mind that it costs a vendor a lot of money to respond in person to an RFP; if a successful proposal would represent a significant amount of business, the vendor may well send a member of its top-level executive management, as well as a sales rep or two and perhaps one or two members of the technical support and customer service teams. They will spend quite a bit of time preparing their presentation, and will bring handouts and other materials for distribution. To ask a vendor to go to this kind of effort when you have already decided against giving that vendor your business is far worse for the vendor than simply having its RFP rejected early on. Of course, in some cases you may not have much choice—if you are subject to requirements that force you to invite a certain number of vendors and that number is greater than the number of viable candidates, then you will have little choice but to invite a vendor whose services do not seem to match your needs. But insofar as it is possible, you should limit your invitations to those vendors whom you are considering seriously.

Allow some flexibility in presentation format and time allotted. It will be necessary to impose limits on the vendor presentations. However, make sure that you keep those limits reasonable, and that you build in some flexibility to account for the differing needs of the vendors making presentations. It would clearly be inappropriate to allow one vendor two hours to make its presentation and another vendor four hours, for example, but if one vendor has more services to explain than another one does, adjusting the schedules a bit to accommodate that difference is quite sensible. As for presentation format, you will also probably need to impose some common-sense restrictions based on the limitations of your local space and technology resources. Make all these limitations clear at the time that you invite candidates to make presentations. Give them the name of a single contact person whom they can call if they have questions about those restrictions, if they have special equipment needs, or questions about anything else. A week or so before each presentation is scheduled, that contact person should

> **Rule of Thumb:** *Every minute spent double-checking arrangements before the vendor's onsite presentation will save twenty minutes of frenzied activity during the presentation.*

> **Rule of Thumb:** *Have more technical help on hand than you think you will need; it may just be enough.*

probably call the vendor and make sure everything is still on track, to confirm that the vendor understands and is planning to conduct its presentation according to the guidelines you have supplied, and that there are not any special needs that the vendor has not brought up.

Make sure that all key staff attend the presentations. This sounds obvious, because it is. But do not let the obviousness of this principle lull you into thinking that everyone on your staff will recognize it and act accordingly. Those who will contribute significantly to the decision need to be present for all vendor presentations in order for them to be able to judge fairly. Ideally, of course, all affected staff will have a say in the vendor choice, but the reality is that some will have more say than others. There is no way to assure that everyone who might have an opinion will attend every presentation, but those who will play an active and decisive role in the decision-making must be there. You cannot make an intelligent comparison of the candidates if you have not heard all of their presentations.

Make sure you have adequate technical support on hand. It is impossible to overstate the importance of this point. You will have established and double-checked each vendor's technical needs ahead of time and made the necessary adjustments (either to your capabilities or to the vendor's expectations), but during the presentation you need to have a technician near at hand who can attend to the inevitable glitches and crashes. And "near at hand" does not mean "at work that day"; it means either in the room during the presentation or perhaps in the next room. No one—not you, not your vendor—wants to sit around in a conference room for half an hour while someone goes looking for a technician who can help with a malfunctioning projection unit.

4.4 AFTER THE PRESENTATION

When the vendors have all gone back to headquarters and the librarians have retreated to their offices with reams of glossy handouts and perhaps some coffee mugs or tote bags, it is time to start evaluating the responses and the additional information culled from the presentations, and to choose the vendor you wish to work with. The criteria you consider and the decision-making process that you follow will necessarily vary substantially from institution to institution. But once the decision has been made, be sure to do two things:

Notify all contending vendors promptly. This is a matter of simple courtesy. Unless you have specific reasons for delaying the announcement, let everyone involved know the decision as soon as it has been made.

Rule of Thumb: Good vendors thrive on thoughtful criticism; bad ones resist and resent it.

Provide feedback to all participants. When you send letters or have telephone conversations to notify the competing vendors of your decision, take the time to give each vendor (including the winner) an analysis of both its weaknesses and strengths. To those vendors that were not chosen, offer specific reasons for the decision you made. Do the same for the winning vendor, making it clear that you expect the promises it made to be fulfilled, and that you will be monitoring the vendor's performance carefully to see that they are. Remember that vendors do not want their feelings protected; they want to improve their services and bring them more closely in line with the needs of their marketplace. A vendor that responds with defensiveness or hostility when you point out its weaknesses is, almost invariably, a vendor with which you do not wish to do business.

FURTHER READING:

Kendall, Mark. "The RFP Process: A Book Vendor's Musings." *Against the Grain* 14 (Dec. 2002/Jan. 2003), 82.

Wilkinson, Frances C., and Connie Capers Thorson, *The RFP Process: Effective Management of the Acquisition of Library Materials* (Englewood, CO: Libraries Unlimited, 1998).

Rumph, Virginia A. "Vendor Selection Using the RFP Process: Is It for You? One Library's Experience." *Indiana Libraries* 20 (2001), 26.

5 ESTABLISHING A NEW SERVICE

In some ways, selecting a vendor or service provider (even by RFP) is the easy part. Although RFPs can require a lot of effort and organization, you ultimately get to sit back and let the competitors try to wow you. But once the selection has been made, you will have a lot of work to do before the new services are fully instituted. Depending on the scope of those services, the process may involve many people in the library. In this chapter, we examine the process of establishing a new approval plan, which is one of the most complex projects you will ever undertake with a vendor, but the general principles discussed here will apply equally well to establishing new standing-order, firm-order, subscription or other services.

5.1   SOMEONE MUST BE IN CHARGE

The importance of this principle cannot be overstated. The process of establishing a new approval plan will involve many people and, therefore, many different personalities and perhaps competing interests. In most cases, the acquisitions librarian or head of collection development should be in charge of organizing, planning, scheduling and—perhaps most important—steering the meetings that will take place.

For several reasons, it is not fair to expect the vendor rep to fill this role. First of all, she obviously cannot schedule the meetings and arrange venues for them before her visit. Second, she probably knows little about the personalities involved. But most of all, it is her job to be a "good cop," not a disciplinarian. When a bibliographer gets long-winded in a profiling session or when two employees start arguing during the all-staff orientation meeting, she will need to rely on someone internal to take matters in hand and get the meeting back on track.

Rule of Thumb: If the meeting takes place in the library, someone from the library must be in charge.

5.2 SETTLE YOUR INTERNAL ARGUMENTS BEFOREHAND

Of course, the best way to avoid such scenes is to have them before the vendor rep arrives. The coordinator of the setup process needs to be someone who can anticipate possible sources of internal friction and conflict, and resolve those conflicts to the extent possible before the vendor rep arrives. This is a good idea, in part, because it will help you avoid unseemly displays of animosity in front of your guest. But even more important is the time it will save. Remember one of the cardinal Rules of Thumb of vendor relations: Time with your rep is precious and should not be wasted.

You will see your rep a few times a year, at most. Spend as much as possible of the time you have together doing things that you cannot do when your rep is not present, and spend as little of it as possible doing things that can be done before or after the visit. Fighting over budget allocations or collection focus or work flow details may be very important—but those are fights that should take place either before or after the vendor rep's visit.

5.3 KNOW WHAT YOU WANT AND WHAT IS AVAILABLE

Another task that must be accomplished before the vendor rep arrives is a thorough review of the needs that you want the vendor to satisfy, and of the vendor's service offerings. Do not wait until the rep arrives to decide what your needs are, or to ask her what your options are. Meet with affected constituencies inside the library well before her visit, and establish with them which services you want and how those services should be delivered. Ask her to send you information about those services, and discuss that information thoroughly before her visit. Do you want your books to arrive shelf-ready? Do you want paperback editions when paper and cloth bindings are available simultaneously? Do you need your shipments to arrive on the same day each week? (Do you even want your shipments weekly, or would bimonthly work better for you?) How should your invoices be formatted? These are all very important questions, but there is little reason to spend time on them during your rep's visit. For the most part they can be nailed down well before she arrives, allowing you to make the most of your time with her. The decisions you reach ahead of time may lead to questions for the

Rule of Thumb: *The more decisions you can make before your rep's visit, the more productive your visit with the rep will be.*

rep, but the decisions themselves should be made, to the extent possible, before she arrives.

Prior to the rep's arrival for the profiling session, she will send you materials designed to help you and your colleagues in their preliminary decision-making. It will be worth your time to check in with each of them a few days before the date of the meeting and make sure that they have looked over those materials and made any decisions that it are possible to make beforehand. This will also give you an opportunity to answer questions they might have and to tackle any internal problems before sitting down with the rep.

Some questions to ask (and answer) well before your rep arrives:

• How frequently would you like to receive your shipments?
• Do you want your books to arrive shelf-ready?
• If so, what processing services will you need?
• Do you have special requirements regarding invoice format?
• Will you want to place funds on deposit, or pay invoices as they are generated?
• Does the shipping schedule matter? What day do you prefer to receive shipments?
• When paperback and cloth editions are published simultaneously, which would you prefer?

5.4   PRE-VISIT CHECKLIST

Planning the content of your meetings is very important. Equally important is planning the logistics and structure of those meetings. Do not leave these arrangements until just before the meetings are to take place, or you will find yourself up to your neck in chaos; similarly, do not assume that a single notification or reminder will be sufficient to ensure that all necessary participants will show up. Here is a suggested planning timeline; note that it begins a solid month before the meetings themselves are to take place:

FOUR WEEKS AHEAD

• Schedule a large room for an all-staff orientation session and a small room for meetings with individual librarians.
• Find out how much time each librarian will need. These time slots should generally be either one-half hour or one hour, unless the librarian is responsible for a very large number of subject areas. When the schedule is complete, send a copy to all involved. Expect to make changes over the coming weeks.
• Request and distribute any of the vendor's manuals, worksheets, explanatory documents or other materials that the librarians and staff should review in preparation for the profiling session.
• Arrange for technical support, as needed. At the very least, you will want a computer projection unit for the all-staff meeting and a network connection for the individual meetings.

What should subject specialists do before the profiling session?

- Review their old profiles. What do they want the new vendor to continue to do, and what do they want it to do differently?
- Look over the vendor's explanatory documentation. Is there anything about the services on offer that the librarian does not understand? Can questions about those services be answered before the rep arrives (leaving more time for substantive discussion when the rep is there)?
- Look over the vendor's list of offered services. Are there any new ones that look interesting? Can they be discussed internally to some degree before the rep arrives?

• If you are switching from one approval vendor to another, ask librarians to review the old profiles and make notes on what they want to replicate and what they want to change.

TWO WEEKS AHEAD

- Send a reminder of the meetings to all involved, along with another copy of the schedule. Also remind all attendees to do their homework (e.g., review profiles, look at manuals).
- Double-check to be sure the rooms you scheduled two weeks ago are still scheduled for you.
- Contact the vendor rep; ask if she has any special requirements, technical or otherwise, that you have not anticipated. Send her a copy of the meeting schedule. Give her directions to the library and any information she may need regarding parking.

ONE WEEK AHEAD

- Make lunch arrangements.
- Double-check to be sure the rooms you scheduled are still scheduled for you.
- Double-check to be sure the technical support you have arranged is still committed to you.

ONE DAY AHEAD

- Double-check to be sure the rooms you scheduled are still scheduled for you.
- Double-check to be sure the technical support you have arranged is still committed to you.
- Issue a last reminder to library staff, specifically asking for notification if anyone's schedule has changed

for the following day. Amend the schedule as necessary and send everyone in the library (and your vendor rep) an updated version.

5.5 SET AN AGENDA AND STICK TO IT

Needless to say, every meeting must have both an agenda and a fixed allotment of time. Keeping meetings focused and the schedule reliable may be the most important duty of the librarian in charge. The agenda will help you keep the meeting focused and its participants on track. It may seem nitpicky to worry about a five- or ten-minute overrun, but remember that once you let a meeting run five or ten minutes beyond its allotted time, the only way to make up the deficit is to take away time from the following meeting. If the same thing happens again, you will then be dealing with a ten- or twenty-minute deficit. It is very difficult to reverse that trend, and it is unfair to expect those who come later in the schedule to sacrifice their time.

Luckily, this type of "meeting creep" is preventable. Remember when you applied for your job and the description in the advertisement said that you would need to have "excellent interpersonal skills? "This is where you get to flex them. Here are some nonconfrontational, but effective, sample phrases you can use to get your meeting back under control when an unruly attendee is threatening to drive it off the road:

- "That's a good point, but maybe we should table this particular issue until we have the rest of the committee together."
- "I really hate to interrupt you, but I see that time is running short and we need to make sure we cover all our agenda items."
- "We'd better make this next item quick—the next person is going to be waiting outside in about five minutes."
- "We're just about out of time, but I see we have several more items on the agenda for this meeting. Can any of these be addressed by e-mail later?"

> **Rule of Thumb:**
> *Remember the Gas Theory of Meetings—every meeting will expand to fill the time allotted, and a meeting for which no time limit is set will expand infinitely.*

5.6 BEYOND CONTROLLING THE SCHEDULE

Running a meeting effectively is about more than just keeping a schedule, however. It is also about making sure that the discussion is productive. As mentioned above, you will need to settle (or at least table) internal arguments ahead of time in order to keep those arguments from distracting you from the business at hand when your rep is present. But you will also need to stay alert to digressions that threaten to eat up the time that you need to conduct that business—not harmless, small-talk digressions, but the kind that can really get in the way. When one of your librarians wants to make a speech about the state of the publishing industry, rather than address the specific issues of the profiling process, for example, or one bibliographer wants to gossip about the others, it will be your job to steer the conversation back to a more productive path. The ability to do so in a firm but diplomatic manner does not come naturally to everyone, but it is an acquirable skill.

5.7 BUILD A SHARED VOCABULARY

In Chapter 3 we discussed the importance of having a shared language with your vendor. Defining some elements of that language will be an important part of establishing your new service. Sometimes terms whose meanings are very clear to you will have different meanings to your vendor, and vice versa. It is also important to know the organizational implications of those definitions before you begin doing business together. Let us look in a bit more detail at the list of potentially ambiguous terms that we briefly discussed in Chapter 3:

Account—Does your vendor think of you as a single account, or does it use an account structure that deals separately with approvals, firm orders, and standing orders? Are accounts identified by number? If so, is there a unifying logic or system to them? When you call to ask a question or resolve a problem, will you need to have an account number ready to give the person who answers the phone? Do discount or service-fee structures differ from account to account?

Claim—While the definition of "claim" itself is relatively unambiguous (a claim is basically a follow-up note asking why you have not yet received something), the practice of claiming varies by circumstance. How long after sending a firm order should you wait before submitting a claim? Does the vendor allow you to submit "claims on approval" (whereby you essentially say, "We think this book should have come on our approval plan, and would like to receive it for consideration.")? Should the claiming period for standing orders be different than the one for firm orders? Format is important—are claims issued on forms that look very much like regular orders, and if so, will that be a problem for the vendor?

Status—What do the vendor's status reports look like, and how frequently will you receive them? In what format will they be sent? How are you expected to respond to status reports, if at all? What terms or abbreviations will be used on status reports, and can the vendor offer a glossary of those terms?

Management Report—Do both you and the vendor attach the same meaning to the term "management report?" What information do the reports contain, and how frequently will you receive them? Can they be requested at odd intervals? Will they be sent in print, or via e-mail, or posted to the Web? Are they available in multiple electronic formats?

Firm Order—How does the vendor distinguish between books that are requested as part of the approval plan (perhaps in response to notification slips or forms) and those that are ordered outside of the approval-plan structure? Are they identified by local fund code, by account number, by mode of submission, or by some other mechanism? Does the term "firm order" refer to more than one type of order in either the library's or the vendor's mind?

Profile vs. Plan—In the world of approval services, the terms "profile" and "plan" (and the numbers that often accompany each) can be confusing. The earlier you can alleviate that confusion on the part of your staff, the more pleasant and productive their future telephone conversations with the vendor will be. Is the approval plan itself identified by a unique number? Does that number have a logical relationship to the account number that governs invoicing for the approval plan (or plans)? Under what circumstances do you need to have these numbers handy? What is a "subprofile," and how does it differ from a "profile?"

Series/Serial/Continuation—Even serials librarians and catalogers sometimes wrestle with the relationship between these terms. Throw an approval plan into the equation and things only get fuzzier. In most approval plans, it is possible either to exclude series or to include them, overriding the normal terms of inclusion or exclusion for your approval plan in the process. But what about annuals? Where does the vendor draw a line between serials and periodicals? Will the vendor actively pursue complete fulfillment of series covered on approval, or will it only include those volumes or issues that happen to come through the approval pipeline (usually it is the latter—if you want more exhaustive coverage you will need to place the title on standing order outside of the approval plan and take a lower discount in return for the higher level of service).

All of the above are terms which the acquisitions or serials staff should review with your sales rep, to make sure that their meanings are understood and mutually shared. Once your staff and the vendor's staff agree on the meanings of these terms , make sure you disseminate that information to all who will be dealing with the vendor's outputs—especially subject specialists. In addition, this is a good time for both parties to ask each other about unique terms that are commonly used in their respective organizations.

5.8   INTRODUCE, INTRODUCE, INTRODUCE

Your vendor rep needs to know who is who, and who does what in your organization. It will save both of you lots of time and frustration in the future if these functions are made clear at the beginning of your relationship. In particular, make sure that your rep knows which members of the staff should be the primary contacts for:

- Questions about shipping
- Technical issues related to shelf-ready services
- Profile changes
- Invoicing concerns
- Financial questions
- Complaints
- Questions about orders

It is also worth noting that people generally work better together who, to some degree at least, know each other and have had some personal interaction. Ideally, your entire staff would personally meet with the vendor's entire customer service staff before services are initiated. For obvious reasons, this is usually impossible. But you can request that your sales rep bring your library's primary customer-service person with her when she comes to establish your new approval plan, and you can make sure that they both be introduced to as many of your staff as is practical. Where this is not possible, you should request a full list of the customer-service staff with an organizational chart. This information can be very valuable in those situations where the nature of the problem does not make it clear whom you should call, or when your regular contact person is unavailable.

FURTHER READING:

Nardini, Robert F. "The Approval Plan Profiling Session." *Library Acquisitions: Practice & Theory* (Fall 1994), 289.

6 NEGOTIATING TERMS OF SERVICE

An important part of setting up new services with your vendor is negotiating the terms that will govern them. Not all of those terms will require extensive negotiation, of course. Many of the details of doing business with a vendor will be settled by a simple expression of preference on your part or the vendor's: how invoices are arranged and sent, how frequently you will receive shipments, whom you should call with particular types of questions or problems—these are not questions that will require much argument or negotiation. But other issues, such as how much your discount will be, how long invoices may mature before payment is due, under what circumstances you will be allowed to return books—may require some haggling and compromise. In this chapter we will discuss some of these issues.

6.1 DISCOUNTS AND SERVICE FEES

Of all the terms of service you will negotiate with your vendors, discounts and service fees have the most potential for causing friction and dissatisfaction. Before we address the variables that affect discounts and service fees, we should define those terms and explain when you will deal with each.

THE BASIC RULE: DISCOUNTS FOR BOOKS, FEES FOR SERIALS

In general, you should expect book vendors to offer you a discount when you buy books through them, and you should expect to pay subscription and standing-order vendors a premium for doing business with them. (When you order directly from publishers, you will usually, though not always, simply pay list price.)

This difference in pricing relates to the fact that subscription agents are providing more service than booksellers typically do. Management of a magazine or journal subscription is an ongoing process involving not only the repeated acquisition, processing, and shipment of issues, but also the (sometimes nearly constant) monitoring of publication patterns and claiming of issues that are late or miss-

Rule of Thumb: *You will get a discount for ordering books through a vendor, and you will pay a service fee for ordering subscriptions through a vendor.*

ing. For this reason, subscription agents generally charge a fee on top of the price of the subscription. For the same reason, while book vendors will often provide standing-order services for books in series, they will usually provide them at a smaller discount than what they offer for monographic services, and sometimes they will not offer any discount at all for those services.

HOW DEEP THE DISCOUNT OR HOW STEEP THE FEE?

What constitutes a reasonable discount or service fee will vary greatly depending on circumstances. However, the factors that determine a reasonable discount or fee are predictable, and include the following:

Volume of business. In general, the more business you do with a vendor, the less it should cost you. On the book side, this means that if you did $150,000 worth of business with a vendor last year and plan to do $300,000 worth of business this year, you should get a deeper discount this year than last. (Your vendor may put you back at the old discount level, of course, if at the end of the year it turns out that your purchases were actually closer to $150,000 than $300,000.) On the serials side, it means that if you significantly increase the number of subscriptions you have with your vendor, you should see a decrease in your service fee. While volume of business is not the only factor affecting discount, it is always a significant one.

Rule of Thumb: *The more business you do with a vendor, the less it should cost you.*

Publisher "mix." Especially when dealing with book vendors, your discount may be significantly affected by the mix of publishers whose books you order through the vendor (or include in your approval profile). To understand how the mix of publishers on your approval list affects your discount, you must realize that a vendor's profit margin is in the difference between the price they pay publishers and the price at which they sell to customers. Not all publishers offer the same discounts to vendors. If a vendor agrees to give your library a 12 percent discount on approval books, and the majority of the publishers covered by your approval profile only give the vendor only a 20 percent discount, the vendor only has 8 percent of list price to pay its expenses and realize a profit. Given this narrow profit margin, you can be sure that your discount is not ever going to get much deeper than 12 percent. (In some cases, the publisher-to-vendor discount may be so low that the vendor offers you no discount at all.) But if you expand your profile to include lots of books from publishers that give your vendor a 30 percent or 40 percent discount, you can make a strong case for a deeper discount from the vendor. When you are negotiating discounts, talk about publisher mix and ask for advice on how you can make the mix of your approval profile or firm orders more conducive to a deeper discount for your library. It will not always be either possible or desirable to add a particular publisher to your profile, but you need to know what your options are.

Deposit accounts. One of the best ways to enhance your discount with either a book or serials vendor is to put money on deposit. This will not always be allowed, especially for state or municipal institutions; before establishing a deposit account with one of your vendors, make sure you are familiar with the rules that govern your institution. But if it is allowed, you can essentially treat your vendor as a bank: if you plan to do, say, $50,000 worth of business with your vendor in the coming year, you can simply write the vendor a check for $50,000 when you get your budget allocation at the beginning of the fiscal year. Then, instead of getting "live" invoices with your shipments throughout the year, you will get statements indicating how much money remains in your deposit account. In return for having access to your money ahead of time, the vendor will either deepen your discount or add interest directly to your account balance; the discount enhancement or interest credit will increase with the size of your deposit. If you are very lucky, the rules under which you work will allow you to put windfall allocations into a deposit account with a vendor and leave them there as a hedge against future budget cuts.

WHAT IS A "WINDFALL ALLOCATION?"

The phone call that librarians both yearn for and dread is the one that sometimes comes right at the end of a budget year, or sometimes several days into a new budget year. The person calling may be your library director or perhaps the provost or a vice president (this situation arises most often in academic institutions), and the gist of the question is usually "How quickly can you spend [a very large sum of money]?" Why does this happen? Sometimes academic or administrative departments fail to expend their entire budget allocations by the end of a fiscal year, and the college or university is stuck with money that has to be spent, and spent quickly. The administration may turn to the library, knowing that the library knows how to get orders processed and invoices paid quickly, and may have a wish list of expensive items that it cannot usually afford. Windfall allocations offer a good opportunity to buy that rare book that Special Collections has always wanted, or to buy more back issues in an online journal database. The best scenario is one that allows you to put the windfall money into a deposit account with one of your vendors, and then spend the deposit slowly over the course of the coming year. This is not always allowed. However, your answer to the question, "How soon can you spend this money?" should always be, "As soon as you need me to." Never refuse to take money when your administration offers it. There is almost always something you can spend it on, and quickly.

However, you should take care: remember that the money you place on deposit is only as safe as the company that holds it. Many librarians have bitter stories to tell about the events of 2002, when a major subscription agent went out of business with little warning and took with it the deposited funds of many libraries, some of them in the amount of several hundred thousand dollars. As of this writing, it was not yet clear whether any of those libraries would recover any of that money, or continue to get all of the journals they had paid for up front. The benefits of establishing a deposit account can outweigh the risks, especially if your vendor has a long and solid financial history and, especially, if the company is bonded. But you should be sure that you know what you are getting into.

WHAT DOES "BONDED" MEAN, AND WHY DOES IT MATTER IF YOUR VENDOR IS BONDED?

There are several different types of bond, but in this context we are talking about a kind of "surety bond"—a promise made by a third party that your vendor will live up to its obligations. That third party will be an insurer or bank that agrees to cover your losses in the event that the vendor suddenly goes out of business or otherwise becomes unable to give you the services for which you have paid. It does not cost your library anything; bonding is paid for by the party being bonded.

While it is worthwhile to know whether each of your vendors is bonded, it is most important when you are dealing with vendors to which you plan to give a large amount of money before they provide the services for which you are paying. For example, if you pay a very large invoice to your serials vendor at the beginning of the subscription year to cover the cost of periodicals that will be provided throughout the year, or if you put a large amount of money in a deposit account with your book vendor to be drawn on as needed, you are essentially investing those large amounts of money in the vendor's ability to provide those goods and services. If the vendor is not bonded and goes out of business one or two months into the year, you may end up losing some or all of that money. A surety bond gives you some insurance against that loss.

Four factors that affect the cost of doing business with a vendor:

- Volume of business
- Publisher "mix"
- Use of deposit accounts (and their size)
- Special services

Special services. If you have your subscription agent or book vendor perform certain extra services (such as physically processing your books or journal issues), that will increase the actual cost of each piece even if it does not technically affect the discount. But of course, if your vendor performs those services for you it will free up your staff to do other things, and that benefit may be significant.

6.2 STATUS REPORTS AND CANCELLATIONS

After you submit an order, you should expect one of two things to happen within a few weeks: either the item you have requested will arrive, or the vendor will send you a status report that explains why the item has not arrived. When you are setting up a new relationship with a vendor, make sure you know how soon after your initial order you should expect to see a status report, and how frequently reports will be sent after that. (Remember that you will sometimes receive several status reports before you get the item you ordered, especially if you submit your order before the item has officially been published.)

Most vendors will cancel your order automatically after you have received a certain number of status reports or the order has stayed open for a certain period of time. Make sure that you know what your vendor's standard practice is in this regard, and if it does not meet your needs, ask for an adjustment. You vendor should be able to adjust its policy for you, and you may want the arrangement to vary depending on the type of material ordered—for example, you would be wise to leave orders for foreign publications open longer than those for domestic publications, since it will almost always take your vendor longer to get a foreign publication than a domestic one. If you are ordering out-of-print books from a specialist vendor, it will usually make sense to leave open orders in place for a very long time (perhaps indefinitely, with an annual review of all open orders), since out-of-print books will appear in the marketplace at unpredictable intervals.

6.3 ARRANGING PAYMENT

Book invoices. In general, you will pay for books as they are shipped to you (or their cost will be deducted from your deposit account balance). This is true for books sent in response to firm orders, for approval-plan shipments and for most standing orders. In the business world, the most common arrangement is for invoices to come due at "net thirty," meaning that the balance (or "net amount") of the invoice is due thirty days following the invoice date. Of course, the date on the invoice will be the day the invoice was created, not the day the invoice is received in your library. Thus, an invoice that is created on July 1 and put into the mail on that day may reach your library on July 8, and will probably have a due date of July 31. This means that you have twenty-three days to process the invoice and get a check into your vendor's hands.

Serials invoices. Serials invoices are more complicated than monographic invoices. For one thing, by their nature, serials invoices are generated at regular intervals—monthly, semi-annually, annually—rather than once. In other words, when you buy a book you buy it once, pay the invoice, and the financial transaction is over. However, when you purchase a subscription you are requesting an ongoing service for which you will pay every year. Thus, instead of paying a single invoice you will pay an annual invoice; this is usually called a "renewal invoice," and renewal invoices will come at different times and in different ways depending on whether you have a single subscription with a publisher or hundreds of subscriptions with a subscription agent. If you have a single, direct subscription with the publisher, you should expect your renewal invoice to arrive about a month before the end of the subscription period. If you have many subscriptions with an agent, however, your invoice will be sent much earlier; this is because your staff will need time to review and process all of the subscription renewals in your local system. Some titles on the invoice will usually need to be cancelled, a process which takes time as well.

Invoices for processing. If your book or serials vendor is providing physical processing services in addition to the books or serials themselves, you will usually have several invoicing options:

- Add the cost of processing to the price of each title
- Make the cost of processing a separate line item at the end of each invoice
- Receive a separate invoice for the cost of processing

If local policy requires you to pay for processing from a different fund than that used for purchase of the materials themselves, then you will probably need to take the third option listed above. Otherwise, your choice will usually simply be a matter of preference based on your local work flow and practices.

Negotiating invoicing periods. While most vendors prefer a thirty-day payment schedule for their invoices, you do not always have to go along with their preference. At many academic libraries and libraries that are part of a large state or municipal administrative structure, the

---

Three basic ways to arrange processing payments on your invoices:

- Add the cost of processing to the price of each title
- Make the cost of processing a separate line item at the end of each invoice
- Receive a separate invoice for the cost of processing

host institution's accounting office will be separate from the library itself. When the library and accounting office are separate, it can take days or even weeks for an invoice to be received, verified in the library, sent to the accounting office and processed there, and for a check to be cut and sent to the vendor. If this describes your situation, you should talk to your vendors about changing their invoicing terms to net sixty or ninety, or at least make sure that you will not be penalized for paying invoices late (as long as they are paid within a reasonable period). Many vendors will agree to extend the due date on your invoices as a matter of course. Others will tell you that they do not have the option of changing the formal due date, but will grant you a grace period. In this case, you need to make sure that you get such an agreement in writing; you do not want to be in a position of having to argue your case all over again when the sales rep who made the agreement leaves the company and is replaced by another one. And in some cases, of course, the vendor will insist that thirty days is all you can have. In those cases, you will have to make some hard decisions: Is it possible to handle this vendor's invoices in a special manner that will get them processed faster? Are the late fees low enough that they are not worth worrying about? Does the vendor have a competitor that provides equally good service and will be more flexible? Obviously, the answers to these questions will vary depending on your situation.

Watch out for early invoices. Vendors that sell their content by subscription or by annual access fee (for online products) will sometimes send renewal invoices well in advance of the actual renewal date. This is a mixed blessing. On the positive side, it gives you plenty of time to get the invoice processed. On the negative side, you do not necessarily want to pay an invoice too early—for example, some publishers have been known to send renewal invoices for individual online databases as much as six months early, in an attempt to get the library's renewal locked in early in the year (and perhaps before the library would usually examine its online holdings to see what it wishes to keep or cancel in the coming year). When invoices are this early, it rarely makes sense to pay them when they arrive. Remember that while you may have to compromise on due dates, you do not have to let the vendor's preference determine when you are invoiced for a renewal. If a vendor or publisher sends you a renewal invoice more than one or two months before the annual expiration date, let your rep know that you are going to discard or disregard that invoice, and that her company should send you a new one at a more reasonable point in the subscription year. If you have no sales rep, which will often be the case when dealing with small publishers, speak with someone in the vendor's accounts receivable department.

> **Rule of Thumb:** *Do not pay a renewal invoice that comes more than sixty days before the actual renewal date.*

6.4 RETURNS

Returns often become a point of contention between libraries and vendors, but they do not need to be; you can establish policies ahead of time that will cover almost any contingency.

Obviously, a basic feature of an approval plan allows you to return books for any reason (or no reason), as long as they remain in saleable condition; the same is generally true of books received in response to individual firm orders as well. But this means, of course, that if you receive an approval book with any kind of physical processing, you will not be able to return it to the vendor unless the book was sent to you in error. Does this mean that books sent on approval with physical processing are not really sent on approval at all? That is correct. Keep this peculiarity in mind when you are deciding to institute physical processing of your approval books. A thorough review of your profiles before beginning a program of physical processing is always highly advisable.

Also bear in mind that your vendor will probably not be thrilled if you keep a book for several months before deciding to return it, even if the book is not processed and it remains in saleable condition. Clarify with your vendor ahead of time how much time you have to make returns.

FURTHER READING:

Walther, James H. "Negotiating Strategies with Library Vendors." *The Bottom Line* 12 (1999), 51.

7 NEGOTIATING A LICENSE AGREEMENT

7.1 WHY YOU NEED TO PAY ATTENTION TO LICENSE AGREEMENTS

License agreements have existed for years, of course. You probably encountered them most regularly as slips of paper that fluttered out of the box when you brought home a new version of Windows, or as annoying pop-up windows that you saw whenever you registered to use a web site such as Hotmail or Expedia—the ones that require you to click on a button that says, "Yes, I've read and understood and agree to the terms of use for this site" (even though you had not read them at all).

But over the last ten years, as libraries have invested more and more money in online products, license agreements have become something that all libraries take much more seriously. Generally, the license agreements that attach to online databases and journal packages must be signed, which makes them binding contracts. (The ones that say "By using this product you are agreeing to the following terms" are referred to technically as "contracts of adhesion," and are not usually legally binding except in those states that have adopted the Uniform Computer Information Transactions Act, or UCITA.) This means that librarians must read and understand them, and must be willing to abide by their terms. It also means that librarians are regularly put in the position of negotiating the terms of license agreements with vendors and publishers.

WHAT IS UCITA?

The Uniform Computer Information Transactions Act is a law intended to change the copyright rules to reflect the new realities of the Internet age. Its provisions are quite controversial. One of the proposed changes that most disturbs librarians is the added weight UCITA would give to what are commonly known as "shrinkwrap" licenses—those contracts that you typically find in software packages that say "By using this product, you agree to the following terms." Standard contract law says that a contract is not usually binding unless both parties have a chance to negotiate the terms and they both affirmatively agree to them. Under UCITA, "shrink-wrap" licenses would have much more legal force—even if they are hidden within the package so that you cannot see the terms until you have obligated yourself to abide by them.

UCITA has many other aspects, of course, and there are arguments both for and against its passage. For a good summary of the arguments against UCITA, see the Association of Research Libraries' web site at http://www.arl.org/info/frn/copy/ucita.html. For arguments in favor, see the Software and Information Industry Association's web site at http://www.siia.net/sharedcontent/govt/issues/ucita/summary.html. As of this writing, UCITA has been adopted by only two states: Virginia and Maryland.

If you are an acquisitions or serials librarian, you may be charged with reading and negotiating the terms of license agreements, but you probably do not sign them yourself; the signatory of a license is usually the library director or perhaps another high-level administrator. In this chapter we will discuss some of the basics of license negotiation. However, anyone who is going to be involved with license negotiation on anything like a regular basis would be well advised to attend the workshops offered by the Association of Research Libraries. (For more information on these workshops, see http://www.arl.org/arl/workshops.html.)

7.2 THREE CATEGORIES OF LICENSE TERMS

As you examine the terms of a license agreement, you should mentally place each of those terms into one of three categories:

1. Acceptable
2. Undesirable but possible
3. Impossible

Acceptable terms, obviously, are those which are both legally permissible and institutionally agreeable.

Undesirable terms are those to which your library is technically free to agree, but which you do not want to accept, either because the requirements are technically impossible to meet or because the terms place an unacceptable burden on the library staff. Common examples of such terms may include the institutional assumption of responsibility for user behavior, inflexible payment terms, confidentiality clauses.

Impossible terms are those to which your library **may not** agree, either because of institutional policy (in the case of private institutions) or state law (in the case of public ones). For instance, most state institutions are forbidden by law from indemnifying vendors against third-party claims or from submitting to the jurisdiction of another state.

Your goal in license negotiation is to take all of those terms that fall under categories 2 and 3 and either eliminate them or change them so that they become acceptable. Vendors and publishers are amenable to this process in varying degrees, but few will refuse to adjust or eliminate license terms to which a library simply may not agree. For example, if you work for a state institution and the law forbids you from agreeing to an indemnification clause, you have only two choices: eliminate the clause or reject the product. Vendors will almost always prefer to keep the sale and forego the indemnification. There is a lesson here: **State law is your friend.** It gives you a tremendous amount of leverage to be able to say, truly, that your hands are tied. (If you work for a library that serves a private institution, the policies of that institution may have the same effect.)

Things get more difficult, however, when the license term in question is one to which your library has the legal option of agreeing, but which is unreasonable. This turns out to be a potentially huge category, one which can itself be broken down into three rough subcategories:

a) Terms to which only a fool would agree;
b) Those which are unreasonable in theory but not necessarily odious in practice;
c) Those which are worth resisting, but not worth walking away over.

How undesirable terms are distributed among these three subcategories will vary somewhat from library to library and from product to product. For example, faced with an online product that will be used by a wide variety of patrons and a license term that says, "The library will

Three categories of undesirable license terms:

- Terms to which only a fool would agree
- Those which are unreasonable in theory but not necessarily odious in practice
- Those which are worth resisting, but not worth walking away over

assume legal responsibility for the behavior of all users," only a truly foolhardy librarian would agree. On the other hand, if the product is only going to be used in-house by a relatively trustworthy subset of the staff (for whose behavior the library is probably liable to some degree anyway), it might be worth considering going ahead even if the publisher refuses to alter the terms.

7.3 BEWARE THE SIX LICENSE TERMS OF DEATH

Even though there will be some variation from institution to institution as to which license terms are completely unacceptable, which are grudgingly acceptable, and which are perfectly fine, there are a few license terms to which no library should ever agree:

Indemnification. Many of the license agreements you encounter will include language saying that the library indemnifies the licensor against the claims of third parties based on misuse of the product by library patrons. If you agree to that language, it will have many troubling implications. Here is one potential scenario: One of your patrons takes information from one of your databases and publishes it as if it were his own. The copyright holder sues the database provider for making the information available to the patron. The database provider points to the license agreement and says, "It is not our responsibility. The library that served this information to the patron has indemnified us against claims such as yours." In other words, by indemnifying the database provider, you essentially become that company's legal insurance policy, and you become the object of the copyright holder's lawsuit. Luckily, if you work for a public institution it is almost certainly illegal for your institution to undertake that responsibility, and the indemnification is unlikely to stand up in court, even if you or your director had signed the license agreement. But it is still well worth your effort to watch for such language and take it out. And remember that most private institutions do not have the same protection as public ones—if an authorized signatory agrees to provide indemnification to a publisher, it is done.

Library Responsibility for Users' Behavior. This is closely related to the indemnification issue, but is often mentioned separately in license agreements. Except in extremely rare circumstances (such as a product that will remain under the library's tight control and will be used only internally), you should never agree to take responsibility for someone else's use of the product—especially not several thousand other people's use of it. No library can guarantee that all of its users will behave legally (or even appropriately), and one of the cardinal rules of contract negotiation is that you do not promise to do something you cannot do.

Unreasonable Termination Rights. Beware any license that allows the content provider to terminate the agreement for "any" breach of its terms, especially if that termination means the cancellation of the agreement with no refund. Just as the library should not have the right to terminate the agreement and demand a full refund in the event of a temporary lapse in service, so the provider should not have the right to cancel access with no refund in the event of a single user's breach of the access terms or a slightly late invoice payment. Instead, the license should say that *either* party has the right to terminate the agreement in the event of a *material* breach of its terms by the other party—and in the event that the breach is not cured within a reasonable period of time after notification by the affected party. (Depending on the nature of the product, a reasonable period might be anywhere from seven to thirty days.)

Jurisdiction. Most license agreements include a note at the end specifying a state (and sometimes a county as well) under whose laws the terms of the license are to be understood, and in whose courts any action resulting from breach of the license will take place. This will, invariably, be the state and county in which the vendor's headquarters is located. No library should agree to this, and again, state institutions are generally not allowed to. In the highly unlikely—but not impossible—event of a lawsuit or criminal trial based on some breach of the license agreement, it will be a huge burden on your institution's legal staff to travel to the provider's backyard throughout the course of the trial. The wise librarian will insist either that the jurisdiction language be changed to its own backyard, or (even better) that it simply be taken out altogether. It really is not necessary that it be included at all; in the event of legal unpleasantness, the attorneys for both parties can work out jurisdictional issues themselves.

Complete Disclaimers of Warranty. It is common practice for a content provider to disclaim all warranties in regard both to the accuracy of the information provided in the product, and also in regard to the product's "fitness for a particular purpose" or even its basic functionality. These disclaimers usually consist of one or two paragraphs written in capital letters, and they are so common in license agreements and terms-of-use documents that it is very easy simply to overlook them. With license agreements, however, especially for very expensive products, it is essential that you examine this language closely. Does the disclaimer say, in effect, that even when the library has paid for the product the provider is not required to provide it? (Do not laugh—many of these disclaimers say exactly that.) If so, the language should be changed. One easy way to fix an overly sweeping disclaimer is to add

The Six License Terms of Death:

- Indemnification
- Library responsibility for users' behavior
- Unreasonable termination rights
- Jurisdiction
- Complete disclaimers of warranty
- Unilateral alteration of license terms

a sentence like this at the end of the section: "Notwithstanding the foregoing, Licensor warrants that the Product will conform broadly to its advertised characteristics."

Unilateral Alteration of License Terms. This may sound obvious, and actually, it is: no contract should say that one party is free to alter the contract's terms after the contract is signed without the agreement of the other party. After all, the whole idea of a contract is that it binds both parties—and a contract that may be changed after the fact by one party obviously has no binding effect on that party. This fact is so obvious and basic that it should come as a shock that anyone would write a contract that says otherwise. And yet you will encounter such contract terms on a regular basis while negotiating license agreements.

There are two acceptable ways to change such language:

1. Change it so that any alterations to the license agreement must be agreed to in writing by both parties before becoming a binding part of the agreement. This is the best solution.

2. Change it so that the licensor is required to notify the licensee of any changes it makes to the license terms, and the licensee has the option of terminating the agreement if the changes are unacceptable. In such a case, the licensee should receive a refund prorated to the term remaining in the contract. This is not an ideal solution, but it will be acceptable in most cases.

7.4 BE ASSERTIVE BUT REASONABLE

The cardinal rule of vendor relations is especially applicable in the case of license negotiation. Being assertive means making sure that you get clear answers to your concerns and questions about the agreement. It means that if you raise a concern about a term in the license and the person to whom you are speaking does not take that concern seriously or is not in a position to resolve it, you insist on speaking to someone else.

Being reasonable, on the other hand, means being aware of the vendor's or publisher's legal exposure and financial realities. While you should insist on some kind of guarantee that the product will do what the seller says it will, you should not insist on specific and ironclad warranties. While you should never submit to the jurisdiction of another state (even if you work for a private institution), there is probably no reason to insist that the vendor submit contractually to yours, either.

7.5   WHEN TO BE EXTRA ASSERTIVE

While negotiating license agreements, you will occasionally encounter situations in which you must take special care to be assertive. Some of them are:

The "Wink, Wink" License Term. Beware the vendor rep who tells you that although the license agreement says X, what everyone understands is that it really means Y. In a situation like this, your response should be simple, direct and firm: "If we all understand that the license means Y, but it actually says X, then we should change it so that it says Y."

The "I'm Not Authorized To Discuss This" Response. Often you will call a vendor to negotiate a license agreement and the person you catch on the phone is not the one who is authorized to discuss license terms. This person may try to dissuade you from going further. Do not let her. You may have to start climbing the hierarchical ladder, which can be awkward, but if you do so you will usually eventually reach someone who can negotiate with you. Or you will not, in which case there is a good chance that you do not want to do business with the company in question.

The "You've Got To Be Kidding Me" Response. Sometimes (though not as often now as in the early 1990s) a vendor will try to intimidate you into leaving the license alone by strongly implying that only worrywarts and those who are anal retentive worry about license terms. If a publisher or vendor tries to pressure you to "just relax," your response should be simple: you will be happy to relax if the vendor will, in turn, relax about requiring you to sign the agreement. If the publisher insists that you sign, then you will insist that the terms be negotiable.

> **Rule of Thumb:** *Legally, the license means what it says, not what you and sales rep agree it "really means." If you cannot agree to the terms **as written**, do not sign the license.*

> **Rule of Thumb:** *If the license is important enough to the company that you have to sign it in order to get the product, then it is important enough to negotiate.*

7.6   PICK YOUR BATTLES

Balancing assertiveness and reasonableness also means knowing which terms are deal breakers and which are not. If the publisher is going to insist on indemnification and you are legally forbidden to agree, you will have no choice but to walk away—but what if the publisher insists on thirty-day payment terms (which are often impossible to meet in large institutions with centralized accounting departments), or on keeping the pricing and terms of the license confidential? Whether you agree to terms such as these will depend primarily on how badly you need the product in question and how flexible your host institution will allow you to be.

FURTHER READING:

Alford, Duncan E. "Negotiating and Analyzing Electronic License Agreements." Law Library Journal 94 (Fall 2002), 621.

Davis, Trisha, and John Joseph Reilly. "Understanding License Agreements for Electronic Products." The Serials Librarian 34 (1998), 247.

LIBLICENSE-L Archives (http://www.library.yale.edu/~llicense /ListArchives/)

8 UNDERSTANDING APPROVAL PLANS

Most academic and large public libraries use approval plans. These may be small and specialized, or they may account for the lion's share of a library's annual collection growth. The books shipped on approval may be unprocessed, or they may arrive shelf-ready, or they may be given some kind of limited physical processing. And the library may have one big approval plan or several smaller ones. There are, however, certain basic principles that you should understand when working with a vendor to establish any kind of approval plan, and we will discuss those in this chapter.

8.1 THE LOGIC OF APPROVAL PLANS

The purpose of an approval plan is simple: to let librarians make as many of the easiest collection development decisions as possible ahead of time, so that they have more of their time available to devote to more difficult work. To illustrate this point, imagine that you work in a music library that serves the undergraduate and graduate population of a major conservatory. Because your collection must support both broad introductory coursework and in-depth research, there are entire classes of new publications that can be defined as "must-purchase" items. For example, you will probably want to buy every new book announced in the Oxford or Cambridge University Press music list, because those are major publishers whose output in music is of great scholarly importance. (Even if one of those presses releases a genuinely bad book, you will still want to have it for purposes of research and curriculum support.) If you work in a small music library that collects heavily in a particular genre of music or area of music research, there may be specialty publishers whose entire output you want to acquire. Even if you do not wish to acquire everything from a particular publisher, it is probably possible to specify particular subject areas that are of automatic interest to you, along with those in which you have a marginal collecting interest and those you wish to exclude.

An approval plan allows you to make such determinations ahead of time. You work with your approval plan vendor to define your "must-purchase" parameters, and the vendor then sends automatically any books that fit within those parameters. You receive and review the books sent, and return any that you do not wish to keep. A well-designed approval plan will allow your subject librarians to spend less time making "no-brainer" decisions and more time putting their expertise to real use—evaluating the collection, searching specialized catalogs, or working with others to build and shape the collection into what your patrons need.

8.2   HOW DO THEY DO IT?

The systems that approval vendors use to select books for their customers are all variations on a basic model that can be most easily explained as a series of filters. First, the library and vendor define a "universe" of books that should be considered for inclusion. This universe is usually defined as a list of publishers—if you think you would ever want to receive a book on approval from a given publisher, then you include that publisher in your approval list. If a publisher is not included in your list, its books will not be considered for coverage in your approval plan (though you will, of course, always be free to order them separately). Once the universe of possible inclusions is defined, the vendor applies other criteria as set out by your approval profile, eventually excluding all titles that do not fit.

Approval vendors generally employ bibliographers to maintain profiles and allocate books to libraries based on them. These will usually be either professional librarians or people with broad experience in the academic book trade and a good understanding of libraries' needs. In most cases, bibliographers actually create descriptions of new books as they arrive at the vendor, and then compare those descriptions to their customers' profiles, sending or excluding books as appropriate. They will invariably have some kind of computer support in allocating books to individual libraries, but in many cases they will exercise a fair amount of individual control and decision-making responsibility in seeing which library gets which books.

8.3   WHAT ARE THOSE OTHER CRITERIA?

To separate books that should not be sent from those that should, an approval plan generally applies criteria that fall into two broad categories: **subject parameters** and **non-subject parameters.**

RUNNING THE APPROVAL GAUNTLET:

Before a book is shipped to your library on approval, it must meet some fairly daunting criteria, which are usually applied in this order:

- Is the publisher included in your press list?
- Are there any blanket exclusion criteria (such as series titles) that apply to this book?
- Are there non-subject parameters (e.g., format, price, place of publication) that disqualify this book for inclusion?
- Does the subject of the book fit your profile?

Only after the book has successfully dodged those bullets, along with any others that you may have built into your approval plan profile, will it actually be sent to your library.

Subject parameters, as you might expect, are concerned with the intellectual content of the book. Your profile might allow shipment of books that are about jazz, for instance, but not books about pop music. Or it might specify broad coverage of books that deal with architecture, but narrow coverage of books dealing with string theory or international commerce. Depending on your vendor and your local preferences, the subject elements of your profile might be defined according to the Library of Congress classification schedule (the same system by which call numbers are determined for books in most research libraries), or by your vendor's locally-developed subject classification system. It will also usually be possible for you to define, within reason, certain overriding criteria of your own that can be used to define exceptions to the broad instructions created in your profile. For example, you might instruct the vendor to exclude all cookbooks except those that deal with a particular style of cooking native to your library's region.

Non-subject parameters (or NSPs) generally address characteristics of the book other than its subject. For example, your profile might specifically exclude books that are collections of previously-published articles, or it might exclude conference proceedings, books that exceed a certain physical size, books that are published in certain countries or books that cost more than you would automatically be willing to pay. NSPs also include parameters that bear more closely on intellectual content (such as the book's difficulty, treatment level or geographical focus) while still leaving aside the question of what the book is actually about. While subject parameters generally require a "yes" or "no" decision in the profile—either you want to get books about garter snakes or you do not—NSPs are usually assumed to be neutral factors unless you specify a restriction.

Other criteria (such as whether the book is a volume in a series, and if so, what kind of series) fall somewhere between the realms of subject and non-subject parameters, but the general concept to understand is that it is possible to include or exclude books from approval coverage based on a wide variety of criteria, which include both subject- and non-subject-related aspects.

8.4   BOOKS IN THE TWILIGHT ZONE

Not all of your profile decisions need to be black-and-white ones that tell the vendor either to send a book or to exclude it entirely. Your approval plan will also specify classes of books that you wish the vendor to tell you about, but which you do not want the vendor to send you unless you say so in response to that notification. The same vendor process that results in shipment or suppression of a particular book can also result in the production of a print form or slip, or some form of electronic notification, that tells you the book has been published, and invites you to request a copy on approval if you would like to examine it.

In the past, these notifications always took the form of paper slips that were mailed to libraries along with the books generated by the approval plan, usually on a weekly basis. The slips were printed on multi-part forms designed to allow you to circulate a copy to a relevant faculty member or subject specialist, retain a copy in the acquisitions department, and return a copy to the vendor as an order, if desired. Most vendors now provide the same information in an online format, making the review and request process much more quick and efficient and less expensive for all involved. As of this writing, the major approval vendors were still willing to send paper notifications to those customers that prefer them, but it is unlikely that they will continue to do so indefinitely.

8.5 TECHNICAL PROCESSING AND BIBLIOGRAPHIC RECORDS

Most approval vendors offer their library customers the choice of receiving books with or without any kind of physical processing. Physical processing can involve any of a wide variety of services, including the application of spine labels with call numbers, hard binding of paperbacks, or the application of barcode stickers and security strips.

A "shelf-ready" book is one which is physically processed to the same extent that your library would have processed it in-house, and which comes with a bibliographic record that is ready for loading into your catalog. Shelf-ready books, as the term implies, can theoretically be taken straight out of the boxes in which they are shipped and put directly into the library stacks. It is worth pointing out, of course, that when books are sent shelf-ready they are no longer sent "on approval" in any meaningful sense of the term—once they have been processed, they cannot be returned to the vendor simply because the library decides it does not need them. However, books that are sent in error, or which have been badly or incorrectly processed, can and should be returned (or a credit given and the book discarded).

8.6   APPROVAL PLAN DISCOUNTS

Discount structures vary from vendor to vendor and from customer to customer. Some vendors will offer deeper discounts on approval books than on books that are firm-ordered, because the process of supplying books on approval is cheaper for the vendor than that of responding to individual orders. Others might offer a deeper discount across the board if you add approval plan services to an existing firm order account. If you are comparing vendors, be sure to get discount estimates based on several possible business scenarios—not just the one in which you are currently working.

As mentioned in Chapter 6, your approval discount will be affected by many different factors, including the volume of business you plan to do with your vendor, the mix of publishers covered by your approval plan, and whether you plan to put money on deposit with the vendor.

FURTHER READING:

Flood, Susan, ed. *Guide to Managing Approval Plans.* Chicago: American Library Association, 1998.

Grant, Joan. "Approval Plans: Library-Vendor Partnerships for Acquisitions and Collection Development." In *Understanding the Business of Library Acquisitions,* ed. Karen Schmidt, 143. Chicago: American Library Association, 1999.

III. BUILDING AND MAINTAINING THE LIBRARY-VENDOR RELATIONSHIP

9 PUTTING OUT FIRES

The relationship between a vendor and a library is like a forest in a number of ways, not the least of which is the fact that fires are inevitable. Your job (and your vendor's) is not really to ensure that fires never happen, but rather to do what you reasonably can to prevent them and, when they do flare up, to keep them from burning out of control.

One thing that you must bear in mind when dealing with vendors is that mistakes are inevitable. (Vendors find that the same is true of dealing with libraries.) All employees are human, most are competent, a few are brilliant, and a few are hopeless. Such has always been the case and always will be in organizations, and the sooner everyone on both sides of the library-vendor relationship recognizes and accepts this simple fact, the more relaxed everyone will be.

For libraries, accepting this reality means recognizing that shipments will sometimes be late, invoices will sometimes be incorrect, and orders will sometimes be filled erroneously or not at all. For vendors, it means recognizing that invoices will sometimes be lost or paid late, orders will sometimes be submitted with incomplete information, and claims will sometimes be sent in error. Each side should expect the other to do what is necessary to minimize these sorts of problems, and when they arise anyway, both sides need to be prepared to solve them quickly, effectively, and amicably.

9.1 BE ASSERTIVE BUT REASONABLE

As it is in so many other areas, a healthy balance between assertiveness and reasonableness is your greatest resource when addressing a service problem with your vendor. It is not only your right, but also your responsibility, to hold your vendors to reasonable standards of service and quality. On the other hand, it is also your job to know where the line is between reasonable and unreasonable demands.

9.2   BEING ASSERTIVE

In this context, being assertive means not hesitating to contact the vendor about a problem, even if doing so might be personally uncomfortable or inconvenient. It means, if a problem recurs several times or if the response you get is unsatisfactory, being willing gradually to take the issue over the head of your sales or customer service representative, climbing higher on your vendor's management ladder until the problem is permanently resolved. It means insisting on a resolution to any reported problem within a reasonable period of time.

9.3   UNACCEPTABLE VENDOR RESPONSES

When you contact your vendor with a problem that appears to be an error on the vendor's part, you will usually get a reasonable response; either the problem will be fixed immediately or you will be told when it will be fixed and will receive periodic updates on the vendor's progress throughout the process. Sometimes, however, the response you get is not reasonable, and it will be your job to insist on something better. Some examples of unacceptable vendor responses are:

No response. The person you need may not be able to answer the phone at the moment you call. There is nothing wrong with that. However, your phone and e-mail messages should be returned by someone within twenty-four hours. Even if the reported problem will take longer than twenty-four hours to solve, you should get a response within that timeframe telling you what is being done and when you can expect a resolution. If the resolution is going to take more than a week, you should expect at least one progress report during the course of that week.

"Our system can't do that." This may be either a reasonable or an unreasonable response, depending on what it is you are asking the vendor to do. For example, a book vendor's system should be able to detect whether you have already ordered a book, and should be able to block a subsequent order for the same title unless you explicitly identify the second order as an intentional duplicate. On the other hand, you obviously cannot expect one vendor to know that you have ordered a book from a different vendor. So while the response "Our system can't do that" is often unacceptable, you should consider it carefully before responding on that basis.

"I can't give you my name." A company that does not allow its employees to identify themselves to customers is one that does not want to be bothered by accountability. The only instance in which this response is acceptable is one in which it is immediately followed by

---

Unacceptable vendor responses to reported problems:

• No response.
• "Our system can't do that."
• "I can't give you my name."
• "I don't know what you're talking about."
• "We can't figure out what the problem is."

"but I can connect you to my supervisor, if you would like to speak with her." Actually, this is partly an issue of accountability and partly one of convenience: you need to know the names of the people in different areas of the company so that you do not have to hunt them down every time you call. You would be wise to keep a list of contacts at each of your vendors close to your phone—in a spreadsheet file on your computer, in a paper desk file, in a Rolodex, or in some other quickly-accessible place near your phone.

"I don't know what you're talking about." There are few experiences in a librarian's life that are more frustrating than that of calling what is supposed to be a customer-support number and reaching someone who knows little or nothing about the product, who does not even understand your question, and who cannot tell you whom to contact for help. This happens most frequently with large companies that have offices in different cities and which may, in some cases, actually out-source their customer support operation to a third party. In cases such as this, your best bet is to call the company's main office and start complaining loudly. If it is possible to threaten the company with loss of your business, do so. Competent customer support is simply too basic a service for a company to neglect.

"We can't figure out what the problem is." This response is blessedly rare, but occasionally an online service provider will tell you that its staff simply cannot figure out why only half of the computers at your site are able to access their database, or your subscription agent might profess utter bewilderment at the fact that you are still not getting the journal issues you have paid for. Mysterious problems do arise, of course; sometimes no matter what you do you cannot find the source of an ongoing problem. But in this situation, the vendor's response should be to find a way around the problem. That may mean having a staff member send you the journal volumes by hand each month; it may mean giving a frustrated faculty member a temporary individual access account until the problem is fixed. The bottom line is that the company has your money, and is responsible for either providing the product or refunding your money. (Unless, of course, you have signed a license agreement saying that the company is not actually required to do so—see Chapter 7.)

9.4   BEING ASSERTIVE WITH SCAMMERS

We will discuss specific techniques for dealing with unscrupulous vendors and unsolicited mailings in chapters 15 and 16. For now, suffice it to say that you should never pay for a service, journal or book that you did not order. Unfortunately, some vendors in the information market-place target their scamming activities directly to libraries. They know that many libraries handle hundreds of invoices each week and do not always read them as carefully as they should. They also know how to phrase their communications in such a way as to give you the mistaken impression that you are under some obligation to them if, for example, you do not return the undesired product promptly. The more success they have in scamming you, the more you will hear from them. Conversely, if you know and stand up for your rights quickly, and if you make it clear to the company not only that you will not be taken in by their scam but that you will also be warning all of your colleagues about them, you will find that the number of scams you encounter grows smaller and smaller over time, as these companies get to know you and decide to look elsewhere for fresh victims.

Luckily, such companies are rare. The vast majority of publishers, vendors and service providers to the library marketplace are trustworthy, competent and pleasant.

9.5   BEING REASONABLE

Being reasonable means recognizing and understanding the limitations under which the vendor must work. It means seeing and comprehending the difference between publisher error and vendor error. It means being willing to work through proper channels within the vendor's organization, which means having an idea of what those channels are and how the organization works. Perhaps most importantly—and we will discuss this in more detail later in the chapter—it means that you consciously proceed from an assumption of good faith on your vendor's part, unless the vendor gives you significant reason to doubt its good faith, in which case you should seriously consider ceasing to do business with it.

9.6   AVOID MAKING UNREASONABLE DEMANDS

As customers, we all need to balance assertiveness with reasonableness when making demands on our vendors. On the one hand, we should not be shy about telling our vendors what we need and when their services do not measure up. On the other hand, the simple fact that we might like to have something does not automatically make it

Unacceptable library demands:

- 24/7 service
- Infinite customization
- Ridiculous return rights
- Unreasonable discounts

a reasonable demand. A few examples of unreasonable library demands (some taken from real life):

24/7 service. This may seem obvious, but you should bear in mind that most vendors observe a forty-hour workweek (at least officially). There will be time-zone differences between your library and some of your vendors; as much as possible, make sure that the work hours of your staff reflect those differences. For example, at the University of Nevada, Reno Libraries, which are in the Pacific time zone, the serials department's invoicing clerk works from 7 a.m. until 3 p.m. rather than nine-to-five. Why? One reason is that the majority of the library's vendors have their corporate offices on the east coast (or in Europe), which means that the early-morning hours are much more productive than the afternoon hours for dealing with invoicing issues.

Infinite customization. It should also be obvious that no vendor can set up a separate work flow for each of its customers. While some degree of customization—well-crafted approval plans, shelf-ready processing that meets local needs, etc.—should be expected, remember that every vendor has to place reasonable limits on that customization.

Ridiculous return rights. In general, you should not consider returning to the vendor or publisher any book that the library staff has physically altered. This may sound obvious, but it is not unheard of for a library to try to return books that it has physically processed. This is only acceptable if the book was sent by the vendor in error. (Of course, if the book itself is has printing errors, such as defective or missing pages, then the publisher should supply you with a replacement copy free of charge.)

Unreasonable discounts. Remember that vendors are trapped between the discounts they can secure from publishers and those they must offer their customers. In some cases—if you are part of a powerful consortium, for example—you may be able to force a vendor to deepen the discount it offers you to the point that it makes little or no profit at all. (If it must keep your business in order to maintain more profitable business elsewhere, the vendor may even be willing to lose money in its dealings with your library.) This may seem like a win for your library, but it is not a healthy arrangement in the long run. Eventually, a vendor that is not making money in the library market will have to stop doing business there, or will be taken over by another vendor that believes it can turn things around. Putting a good vendor in such a position ultimately does libraries more harm than good. It is important that you fight for good pricing; it is also important that you fight fair and avoid actions that are likely to make it impossible for good vendors to do business with you.

9.7 BE CIVIL

When a vendor has messed up your shipment or sent a book you did not order, or when an online journal for which you have paid a tremendous amount of money is suddenly telling your patrons that they need to subscribe in order to access its content, it is only natural to react with irritation. If your goal is to get the problem solved as quickly and effectively as possible, though, you will want to keep that irritation under control. You do not need to pretend that everything is fine, but you do need to avoid saying or doing anything that will get in the way of solving the problem. If you are frustrated or angry, it may be difficult to listen carefully to the vendor's response. Make the effort anyway. There is always the chance that what you think is an error on the vendor's part is actually a misunderstanding on yours, or that what looks like a vendor error actually stems from a library mistake earlier in the process. Your embarrassment in a situation like that will be much less if you take a civil and professional approach.

Here is an example of an unfortunate exchange between an irritated librarian and a vendor. Notice that the librarian sets the tone for the conversation from the moment the vendor answers the phone:

> **Vendor:** Acme Books, this is Helen. How may I help you?
>
> **Librarian:** Helen, this is Bob Pearson at the Brenner University Library. You guys screwed up our shipment last week, and I want to know what's going on.
>
> **Vendor:** Okay, Bob, what's the problem?
>
> **Librarian:** Well, once again you've sent us a book we didn't order. This has really got to stop; this makes three times in the last year.
>
> **Vendor:** Let me see if I can figure out what went wrong. Can you tell me the invoice number and which item on the invoice is a problem?
>
> **Librarian:** I'm looking at invoice number 266298, line 32. The book is called *Diary of a Codebreaker*. This is not anything we ordered, and frankly, I'm pretty sick of seeing these kinds of errors from you guys.
>
> **Vendor:** Hang on a minute, let me pull up the invoice in our system and have a look. (Pause) Ah, I see the problem.
>
> **Librarian:** Well, what is it? What did you guys do?
>
> **Vendor:** Believe it or not, this really is a book that you ordered. What happened is that you placed your order back in May, several months before the book was published. Back then it was called *I Was a Teenage Decompiler*. Just before it was released, the publisher changed the title. If you check the ISBN of this book, I think you'll find that it matches the ISBN of your order number BCN5582, even though the titles are different.

Librarian: (Embarrassed, but still sounding irritated.) Okay, fine. (Pause) Well, I guess that answers my second question, which was why it was taking us so long to get *I Was a Teenage Decompiler*. (Another embarrassed pause.) Thanks.

This librarian made two fundamental mistakes before and during his conversation with the vendor, and he ended up embarrassing himself as a result. These mistakes were:

Starting off with a hostile attitude. Even if he had been right about the vendor's error, there was no need for Bob to start off the conversation in such a hostile way. It was unprofessional and it lessened the likelihood of a constructive exchange taking place. If his rep had gotten prickly and defensive, things could have gotten very ugly, very quickly.

Not doing his homework. Before accusing his vendor of making a mistake, he should have explored other possible explanations for the problem. It would not have taken a tremendous amount of research to determine that *I Was a Teenage Decompiler* had been the prepublication title of *Diary of a Codebreaker.*

Given the choice between those two mistakes, it is probably better to call before doing your homework than to call in a spirit of hostility. The best-case scenario for a librarian who deals with his vendor in a nasty manner is that he will succeed in proving the vendor wrong and both parties will hang up the phone in a spirit of ill will. The worst-case scenario is that he will be proved wrong himself, and he will end up feeling even more stupid than he would have if he had approached the vendor in a more professional manner. In the case above, if the librarian had taken a more professional approach, the exchange would likely have proceeded more like this:

Vendor: Acme Books, this is Helen. How may I help you?

Librarian: Helen, this is Bob Pearson at the Brenner University Library. I'm confused about something in our most recent shipment, and I wonder if you can help me figure out what happened.

Vendor: Certainly. What's the problem?

Librarian: Well, there's a book in this week's shipment that I don't think we ordered. It's line number 32 on invoice number 266298; the title is *Diary of a Codebreaker.*

Vendor: Hang on a second, let me look it up. (Pause) Ah, I see the problem. This is a title change. When you ordered the book originally, back in May, it was tentatively titled *I Was a Teenage Decompiler.* The publisher changed its title just before the street date. You ordered it under the old title on PO number BCN5582.

Librarian: Of course, I should have thought to check that. We'll change our records to reflect the new title. Thanks for the help, and sorry for bothering you over nothing.

> **Vendor:** It was no problem at all. Is there anything else I can do for you?

Notice that in the above exchange, even though the librarian ended up feeling a bit embarrassed about having missed an obvious explanation for the problem, he did not experience the sort of teeth-grinding humiliation that comes from nastily accusing someone of bad faith and then realizing that you were the one in the wrong. That is a feeling that, for most of us, easily outbalances the dubious pleasure of catching someone else in an error and rubbing his nose in it.

9.8   DON'T ASSUME TREACHERY WHEN HUMAN ERROR IS MORE LIKELY

Psychologists tell us that we do not really get angry at people for what they do; we get angry at them for the motivations that we believe led them to do the things we think we are angry about. In other words, if someone cuts your car off on the highway, making you slam on the brakes and skid heart-stoppingly across the road, chances are good that you will react angrily. What an inconsiderate jerk! But if you later find out that the man behind the wheel was rushing his child to the hospital so that she could have an emergency appendectomy, your feelings about the driver instantly change, despite the fact that what he actually did to you is still the same. The difference is that you understand his motivation differently—he was not being inconsiderate and thoughtless after all; he was in a desperate hurry and had more important things to worry about than the social niceties of the road. Presumably, you would have done the same thing in his situation.

What about when your vendor makes a mistake? That certainly does happen, and when it does, you have the opportunity to make certain assumptions about the reason for the error and the motivations of those who made it. The assumptions you can make about such errors are almost infinite in their detail and variety, but they fall into two general categories:

"It must have been an honest mistake" (the Good Faith Assumption). The thinking behind this assumption goes like this: Despite the general good faith of your vendor, there was a glitch in the system, or someone was having a bad day, or someone simply overlooked a detail in some process. The error was unintentional and the vendor is most likely unaware that it even happened. If the vendor were aware, a representative would probably be on the phone with you already, proposing a solution. All you need to do is let your vendor

Rule of Thumb: *Always start with the Good Faith Assumption. Change your assessment as the evidence warrants.*

know what happened and everything will be taken care of, because after all, no one is trying to cheat you; this was just an honest mistake.

"They're trying to cheat me" (the Bad Faith Assumption). The thinking behind this assumption goes like this: Here goes your vendor again, trying to make a buck off your library by any means it can. Those guys think they can sneak little things like this past you and nickel-and-dime you to death because they think you are stupid and not paying attention. Well, you have caught them and you are not going to stand for this kind of nonsense anymore.

The first line of thinking assumes that the vendor is dealing with you in good faith—working hard to give you what you have paid for and looking out for your interests as well as its own. The second assumes that the vendor is dealing with you in bad faith—generally looking for ways to exploit you and only pretending to operate from a position of honesty and goodwill. Now, it is true that there are vendors and publishers who do, in fact, act in the marketplace from a position of bad faith. These vendors should be rooted out, publicly identified and, hopefully, put out of business. It is also true that the majority of publishers and vendors are behaving in varying degrees of good faith. Most of them want to make a profit (and all of them need to establish and maintain a revenue stream), but for the most part they are in the information business for many of the same reasons librarians are: they are interested in their subject areas, they want to contribute to the world of scholarship and human knowledge, they like books, they support literacy and education. None of us should be so Pollyannaish as to assume that our vendors are going to sacrifice their own long-term commercial interest in order to make us happy, but in the great majority of cases we can safely assume that they are not actually trying to cheat us.

Rule of thumb: If your vendor will not tell you what is going on, then you can be sure that what is going on is not good.

Rule of thumb: If your vendor will not talk to you, then you can be sure that things are going on that it does not want to talk about.

9.9 HOW TO TELL WHEN YOU ARE BEING CHEATED

When it is clear that one of your vendors has abused your trust, you should not hesitate to respond firmly. Here are some examples of vendor behaviors that can be taken as, at the very least, strong evidence of bad faith:

Evasiveness. You paid the invoice three months ago, the check has been cashed, but you still do not have access to the online database for which you paid. Your phone calls are met with cheerful but vague assurances that everything is fine and your access will be in place shortly, or that something innocuous has temporarily gone wrong and will be

Rule of thumb: Any company that makes outgoing calls to ask for your money but will not accept incoming calls once it has your money is not a company with which you want to do business.

Rule of Thumb: Every company (and every library) will give you a runaround sometimes. Companies that turn the runaround into an art form are hoping that you will simply give up and let them keep your money.

Rule of thumb: Legitimate vendors and publishers start out polite, and do not get nasty or threatening until all other approaches have failed. Vendors or publishers that are trying to cheat you will resort to threats immediately, in the hope that you will respond to those threats without looking very hard at the merits of their case.

fixed "sometime soon." These are often followed by (unfulfilled) promises that someone will call you back with an explanation.

Unresponsiveness. You call and call and call, and you e-mail and e-mail and e-mail, and no one ever returns your calls or answers your messages.

Inaccessibility. You ask to speak with the person who sold you the product, and the operator tells you that the company's sales representatives "cannot take incoming calls." Or even worse, the company does not offer a phone number at all—only a web-based form, which returns error messages when you try to submit your complaint, or an e-mail address, which returns error messages saying that the "destination mailbox is full," or simply turns out to be invalid.

Suspicious disorganization. You call to ask why you have not received the ten-volume set you ordered and for which you prepaid, and you find that the person who sold it to you has left the company. Her replacement has no record of your order and is not sure whom you should contact to get things back on track. You ask her to transfer your call to the sales manager, and she puts you on hold for fifteen minutes; then your call is cut off. You call back and get her voicemail. You call back again and ask to be connected directly to the sales manager, and you are patched through to someone in the maintenance department. You call back again and the line is busy.

Threatening language. You received an invoice one month ago. You receive a letter after thirty-one days demanding payment and threatening legal action if payment is not immediately forthcoming. (For more on this approach and on how to respond to it, see Chapter 15.)

10 PREVENTING FIRES

In the previous chapter we addressed methods of containing the fires that will inevitably flare up in the course of doing business with a publisher or service provider. In this chapter we are going to back up a bit and talk about ways of preventing those fires in the first place. It is not possible to prevent them completely, of course, but with preparation, the right attitude, and a little common sense, it is possible to make them much less likely.

10.1 PUT YOUR BEST PEOPLE ON THE PHONE

This piece of advice is equally applicable to vendors and librarians, and it hinges on a fundamental reality of providing and receiving services in the modern world: the only interaction you and your staff will have with many of your service providers (or, in the case of vendors, with many of your customers) will be by telephone or e-mail. This means that you need to ensure that those of your staff who interact with your service providers have the following characteristics:

- A pleasant and helpful demeanor
- The ability to analyze situations quickly and accurately
- A thorough knowledge of your organization, its practices and structure
- Patience
- The ability to control a conversation when necessary, without the tendency to do so when it is not necessary
- The ability to express ideas clearly and concisely in writing

Six essential skills and characteristics for working with vendors:

- A pleasant and helpful demeanor
- The ability to analyze situations quickly and accurately
- A thorough knowledge of your organization, its practices and structure
- Patience
- The ability to control a conversation when necessary, without the tendency to do so when it is not necessary
- The ability to express ideas clearly and concisely in writing

For the most part, we hold vendors to a higher standard than libraries in this regard. This is partly because vendors are service providers in a competitive marketplace and must distinguish themselves from their competition primarily by the quality of their service. Also, vendors generally have much more freedom to hire and fire staff than do libraries.

If you are in a situation that requires you to choose an existing staff member as your telephone liaison with vendors and none of your staff fits all of the above criteria perfectly, it may help to think about those criteria in reverse order, using reverse logic. In other words, make sure that you do not put anyone on the phone with vendors who can be described as:

- Impatient
- Easily flustered or confused
- Easily manipulated
- Brusque or unpleasant
- Ignorant of your organization's structure and practices

As in so many areas of vendor relations, truly effective "fire prevention" requires a delicate balance between pleasantness and firmness. A staff member with a short temper can quickly cause tremendous problems; similarly, difficulties can arise just as fast when a staff member is too accommodating or trusting. Consider, for example, the problem of vendors who send unsolicited materials to libraries and then demand payment. Many of these vendors start the process by calling the target library and talking the person who picks up the phone into "approving" the shipment (sometimes by asking the staffer to "confirm" the library's shipping address, and sometimes by convincing the staffer that his or her supervisor "really wants me to get this directory to him fast"). Often these vendors will deliberately target library staff from outside of the Acquisitions and Serials areas, hoping that the person they end up speaking with will be someone who does not recognize the scam pattern. But often they will call your frontline staff, and these employees will need to be tough-minded people who are capable of staying firmly in control of the conversation. In situations such as this, a staffer's pleasantness must be tempered by analytical skill and a hardheaded resistance to verbal bullying or manipulation.

Rule of Thumb: *Make the format of your purchase orders as boringly consistent as possible.*

WHEN CONSISTENCY HURTS RATHER THAN HELPS

When it comes to submitting orders, consistency is almost always the best policy. However, in other contexts it can be a problem. For example, it is essential that your claims and your purchase orders differ very clearly in appearance. The reason for this is fairly obvious when you think about it: a claim that looks too much like an order can easily result in a duplicate order. Many libraries use identical paper forms for both orders and claims, altering only a printed word at the top of the form. To do this is to ask for trouble. If you will be submitting printed claims, use a different ink color from that used for order forms. If that is not possible, use a bright yellow or orange highlighter to mark the word CLAIM at the top of your claim forms. Your goal is to make it as difficult as possible for your vendor's staff to mistake a claim for a second order.

10.2   SUBMITTING ORDERS I: BORING IS BEAUTIFUL

Contrary to what many members of the general public believe, librarianship actually offers many good opportunities for creativity and self-expression.

The design and submission of purchase orders is not one of them.

The purchase orders you send to vendors should not be loose variations on a general theme. They should be, to the extent possible, absolutely identical in every particular *except for the data describing the individual items you are ordering.* To the extent that you are able to maintain this consistency, you will greatly reduce the number of errors your vendor makes in fulfilling your orders.

Why should it matter whether your purchase orders are presented in absolute, mind-numbing uniformity? After all, your vendor is examining each purchase order carefully in order to know what you are ordering, right? Wrong. In fact, your vendor is giving each of your paper purchase orders only the most cursory glance, and is looking for one or two bits of key information—your account number (which identifies your institution and the account to be billed), the ISBN and, for confirmation purposes, the first few words of the title. Most of the other information on your purchase order is of little interest at the point of order receipt (though it may be necessary further down the work flow stream). This is a perfectly reasonable way of doing business—in fact, if you think about it, you would not have it any other way. If your vendor pored carefully over every one of the literally thousands of orders that are received every week, the orders would never get fulfilled. Your job as a customer is to make it possible for your vendor to fulfill your orders as quickly and efficiently as possible, and to make it as difficult as possible for the vendor to misinterpret the information you provide.

There are several ways to achieve this goal:

1. **Use your local system or the vendor's system to submit orders.** If your vendor can accept electronic orders directly from your local library system, use that function. If that function is not available, but the vendor provides an online form for submitting orders, use it. If the vendor provides notification forms or slips that can be returned (or that are linked to online records from which you can submit your orders electronically), use them. Wherever possible, avoid creating your own version of something that the vendor has gone to the expense of providing for you—and, most importantly, which it already understands and is set up to use.

Three steps to foolproof ordering:

- Submit orders through your vendor's online system
- Present all repeated information the same way in every order
- Give all essential information in every order

2. **Present any repeated information the same way every time.** If you are submitting orders using either a locally-produced paper form or electronic message, make sure that the format does not vary from order to order. Your account information, the title and ISBN of the book, the series title and other ordering information should be in the same place on the form and identified by the same language every single time.

3. **Give all essential information in every order.** There are certain pieces of information that you simply must supply in an order so that the vendor can process it. These required elements will vary slightly from vendor to vendor and format to format (serials orders call for different kinds of information from those required for monographic orders, for example), but you can be certain that every order you submit should include all of the following:

   a) ISBN, ISSN or other unique identifier
   b) Title
   c) Your institution's name
   d) Account number to be charged

This is a short list, and you may have noticed that some of the elements librarians usually think of as essential (such as purchase order number, author and publisher) are missing. That is because those elements are not essential from the vendor's perspective, as long as the elements listed above are included and accurate. Publisher name? Not necessary as long as the ISBN and title match. Author? Ditto. Purchase order number? While including a PO number with each order is good library practice, it is not something the vendor normally cares much about or needs in order to fulfill your order.

10.3 SUBMITTING ORDERS II: THE JOY OF AUTOCRACY

All of us understand the value of democracy, and, to the extent possible, most of us want to use democratic processes in the design and implementation of policies in our departments. However, there are areas in which the acquisitions or serials librarian must be willing to dictate. One of these is the question of who may submit orders to vendors or publishers. Consider the experience of one customer service rep:

> I used to get phone calls on a regular basis from a subject bibliographer at a major research library. He had somehow figured out that I was his library's customer service rep, and he would call me in high dudgeon once a month or so, demanding an explanation as to why this or that "absolutely essential" book in his area of expertise hadn't been shipped on the approval plan. I would look at the profile and explain why the book had been excluded, and he would then insist that I send the book as a firm order. I would then have to explain that he needed to submit his request through his acquisitions department, and that just infuriated him: "But I'm the bibliographer for this area, and I know we need this book!" So I would explain that unless an order was created in his library's system, the folks who open up the boxes wouldn't have any way of knowing why the book had been sent to them—in fact, they would assume it had been shipped in error and would probably return it to us. After a few conversations like this he gradually came to understand, and although he still called regularly to find out why a book had not been sent on approval, he reconciled himself to the necessity of ordering through the proper channels.

Few things cause as much confusion and irritation in an acquisitions department as the unexpected appearance of items for which there is no order record. How is one to know the difference between items that have been ordered informally, over the phone or by e-mail, and those that were never ordered at all, but have been shipped in error or as unsolicited mailings? The way to minimize such incidents is to rule the ordering process with an iron hand: make it clear to all in the library that every order *must* be handled through the acquisitions or serials department and a purchase order record *must* be created before it is submitted to the vendor or publisher.

The reason for such a policy goes beyond issues of organization and efficiency. There are also legal ramifications. In Chapter 15 we will discuss in detail the problem of unsolicited mailings and the library's legal rights in regard to such mailings. A consistently successful strategy for dealing with them hinges, in part, on a firm policy of entering all orders in your local system and assigning a purchase order number to each. Without this policy, you will not be able to tell scam artists with confidence that the lack of an order record means that your library did not, in fact, place an order.

Rule of Thumb: Every order you submit, whether by phone, mail, e-mail or electronic interface, should be reflected in your system by a purchase order record.

10.4 KNOW WHO YOUR FRIENDS ARE

When you suddenly lose access to an online database or e-journal, or when the book you receive does not match the one listed on the invoice, few things are more frustrating than not knowing who can actually solve the problem.

Make no mistake, vendors and publishers have an obligation to make it easy for you to figure out the right person to call. Every publisher's and service provider's web site should have, on its first page, a prominently-placed button labeled "Contact Information." That link should lead to a page that clearly indicates not only the company's mailing address, but also e-mail addresses *and phone numbers* for technical support staff (who deal with access and software issues), customer service representatives (who deal with billing, ordering and shipment problems) and sales representatives (who can discuss pricing, consortial deals, new and upcoming products and services).

That said, it is your job, and that of your staff, to gather the above information early on (*very* early on) in your relationship with the publisher or vendor, and to organize it for quick access. Do not assume that if problems arise later in that relationship, it will be easy to determine the proper channels of inquiry for getting those problems resolved. When you place your first order with a vendor or when you initially set up an approval plan or other ongoing service, make sure you get full contact information for those with whom you should be in touch when you have questions or concerns related to each of the following:

- Shipments and invoices
- Orders
- Pricing, consortial deals, new products
- Problems with access to online content
- General service problems

When addressing problems with your vendor, bear in mind that in most publishing houses and vendor offices, the sales staff and customer-service staff operate in parallel worlds. There is communication between them, of course, but like all interdepartmental communication it is usually imperfect. (For a good general model of how sales and service communicate with each other in the vendor world, look at communication between your library's reference and technical service areas.) What this means is that you will do better to call your customer-service rep about shipping errors or fulfillment problems than to tell your sales rep during his semiannual visit. While your sales rep will surely want to be aware of such problems, and will be willing to take note of them and try his best to communicate their essence to those who can fix them, the added layer of communication will tend to make the solutions imperfect. Similarly, you will probably get less-perfect information about pricing options from your customer-service rep (who may know how a product is priced in general, but may not be aware of special deals available to institutions in your category or geographic area) than from your sales rep.

10.5 WATCH YOUR E-MAIL

Although you should insist that your vendors provide you with phone numbers as well as e-mail addresses for those with whom you will need to be in contact, you will probably find that much of your day-to-day interaction with vendors takes place via e-mail. Therefore, it is important that both you and your staff monitor your e-mail regularly, or, even better, constantly throughout the workday.

Is constant monitoring of e-mail reasonable? Yes. Most e-mail systems, even fairly rudimentary ones, offer the option of both audible and visual alert signals to let you know when a new message arrives. With one or both of those functions enabled, you can monitor your e-mail traffic even as you perform other tasks. While those who subscribe to multiple e-mail distribution lists (or even to only one or two high-traffic lists) may find the regular beeps and onscreen pop-ups annoying, that fact may help convince staff to keep those subscriptions to a minimum. The annoyance is a relatively small price to pay for the benefit of being able to stay in touch with service providers on an almost real-time basis as they work on problems you have reported or provide answers that you or others in your library may be awaiting anxiously.

Most library staff—and too many librarians—do not realize that ongoing monitoring of e-mail is desirable. Make sure that your staff does understand that.

10.6 BE ASSERTIVE BUT REASONABLE

When it comes to preventing "fires" in your relationships with vendors and publishers, the essential balance between assertiveness and reasonableness is achieved in the usual ways: by being willing to insist on certain preventive measures and by taking seriously your own responsibilities as a customer. In particular, bear in mind the following points:

- It is your vendor's job to provide you with clearly-marked channels of communication so that you know where to go when problems arise.
    - It is your job to keep that information organized and handy and to communicate it to your staff.
- It is your vendor's job to respond quickly when problems are reported.
    - It is your job to report problems promptly.
- It is your vendor's job to employ personnel that are capable of responding intelligently and knowledgeably to questions from your staff.
    - It is your job to maintain a staff that is capable of asking intelligent and knowledgeable questions of the vendor's personnel.
- It is your vendor's job to grasp quickly the problem you report.
    - It is your job to know what the problem is before you report it (inasmuch as this is possible; sometimes the problem is that you cannot tell what is going on).

Again, none of the measures proposed in this chapter will prevent "fires" from breaking out in your relationships with vendors. But they will help keep the likelihood of such outbreaks to a minimum, and will help you contain and extinguish them quickly.

11 WORKING WITH SALES REPRESENTATIVES

Just about everyone who works in a library acquisitions or serials department will have the chance to work with sales reps at some point. The heads of those departments (along with collection development managers) will have the most frequent direct interaction with them, but when sales reps come to visit they will often ask to tour the relevant departments and talk with front-line classified staff as well, asking whether their companies' services are meeting the library's needs and whether there are problems that need to be addressed.

Your relationship with your sales reps is very important. They will be your source of information about new publications and products and about changes to existing products and services, and they will act as a conduit for your suggestions and complaints. Behind the scenes, your sales reps will often be your strongest allies and most effective advocates with vendors, explaining and championing your needs to those in the company who can make things happen.

Sometimes, and unfortunately, librarians regard sales reps with undue suspicion. To some degree, this is understandable. For one thing, we know that the rep is after our money, and we tend to regard our money as more than just a limited resource—it is also something of a sacred trust, and we do our best to guard it carefully. For another thing, sales reps carry with them the whiff of corporate culture (almost always repellent to librarians); they are usually dressed like business people, and sometimes they may come across as slick and insincere. Worst of all, most librarians know, or at least believe, that their sales reps are being paid substantially more than they are themselves. All of these factors can lead librarians to regard sales reps with skepticism, even suspicion, and to some degree that is healthy.

But it is worth pointing out that at their best, sales reps are similar to librarians in their devotion to the library profession and its ideals; in fact, many are librarians themselves. It is also worth noting that almost all of them work under tremendous pressure and in conditions that can most charitably be described as difficult. All of them deserve our professional courtesy. In this chapter, we will discuss some specific points of etiquette and strategy in dealing with sales reps.

11.1 KEEP YOUR APPOINTMENTS

Basic professional courtesy would dictate that when you make appointments with sales reps (or anyone else, for that matter), you make sure to honor those appointments or let the rep know when it turns out that you cannot.

Why even dwell on such an obvious point? Because, unfortunately, librarians do not always live up to this standard as well as they should. The next time one of your sales reps calls on you, ask for a couple of good stories about librarians who have made appointments and then not kept them. After the standard disclaimers ("I know that you would never do this to me, you and your staff are always wonderful") you will be treated to at least one hair-raising story of a last-minute trip organized at a librarian's request and fraught with weather delays, bad roads and nasty hotel rooms, at the end of which the rep arrived to find that the librarian who demanded the meeting had forgotten all about it and decided to take a week's vacation. Unfortunately, such stories are not as unusual as they should be.

... AND A NOTE TO SALES REPS

You may have noticed this happen before: You have an appointment with a librarian, and, like any good businessperson would, you show up about fifteen minutes early. You would think the librarian would be pleased with your efficiency and punctuality, and yet you notice a distinct look of annoyance flicker across his face as he invites you in, asks you to have a seat and quickly finishes tapping out an e-mail message or sorting through some mail while he makes small talk with you.

The problem is that, as a sales rep, you will mainly be calling on librarians at the managerial level. These are people who tend to be very busy, and whose schedules are sometimes very, very tight. If a library manager has a half-hour gap between the end of his previous meeting and his appointment with you, that half hour will look to him like a golden opportunity actually to get one or two things done—send a few e-mails, return a couple of phone calls, talk to a staffer. If you show up halfway through that precious window of opportunity, the opportunity disappears. He will not get angry at you, because it would be silly to get angry at someone for being punctual, but he will probably not be in the mood you want him to be in when you are ready to begin your pitch.

No one wants you to be late to your appointments, but please, do not show up early unless you have a compelling reason to do so. Just be on time.

But beyond the matter of simply being there when she arrives, there are other, almost equally obvious, elements to a successful vendor visit. In the spirit of emphasizing the obvious, then, here are several specific points to keep in mind when setting up a visit with your sales rep:

Tell your rep where to park and how to find you. Is this her first visit? If so, make sure that she knows how to find the library, where she can park (or where she must go either to register as a visitor or to purchase a parking pass), and how to find your office. Give her this information early on in the planning process—do not make her call you from a cell phone in her rental car while she circles around your library or campus.

Allocate a specific amount of time. Well before the visit, discuss with your rep how much time you have allocated to spend with her. This will help both of you plan the day and will prevent misunderstandings. Do not feel obligated to set aside more time than you can afford, but do plan to make the best use possible of the time you have with your rep.

Tell your staff she is coming. Do not let your staff be surprised by the sudden appearance of a sales rep. Let them know you are planning the visit, and make sure that they are prepared to bring up any issues or concerns they may have. If there are numerous such issues or concerns, include a staff meeting in your agenda, making sure to set aside sufficient time to address those issues.

If you must cancel, give your rep as much warning as possible. The best-case cancellation scenario is one in which an unavoidable conflict comes up at least a week before your rep's scheduled visit. This allows you to contact the rep, apologize profusely, and reschedule. Your rep may end up stuck with a nonrefundable plane ticket, but in many cases the trip will not be a total loss for her—she may have other accounts in the area that she can visit, or at the very least she will be able to plan other uses for that day. The worst-case scenario is one in which you have set an appointment with your sales rep for eight in the morning, and you awake that morning to a family emergency or horrible stomach flu. In cases such as this, there is little you can do to save the situation; however, you can call and leave a message with your staff to pass along to your rep, and you should not fail to do so. By no means should your rep be left wandering around the

---

Preparing for a visit from your sales rep

- Tell her where to park and how to find you.
- Allocate a specific amount of time for the visit.
- Tell your staff she is coming.
- If you must cancel, give as much warning as possible.
- Be punctual.

library, wondering whether you are going to show up and not wanting to leave in case you do.

Be punctual. Like the other points above, this one should go without saying. Your rep's time is as valuable as your own, and squandering someone else's time is deeply inconsiderate, not to mention unprofessional. If you are unavoidably delayed, call your office as soon as possible and leave a message for your rep explaining the situation and indicating when you expect to arrive. If you are delayed and unable to call ahead, when you do finally arrive you should apologize sincerely and briefly—but do not subject your rep to a long and drawn-out explanation, which will likely sound more like a plea for sympathy than an apology. Take responsibility for the delay (even if circumstances were beyond your control) and move forward, salvaging as much of the visit as possible.

11.2 ON THE FLIPSIDE

The flipside of the punctuality issue is, of course, the fact that a sales rep should not show up on your office doorstep without an appointment. In fact, you may wish to establish a policy of refusing to see vendor reps who arrive without appointments. In such a situation, there is no need to offer excuses, to apologize or to pretend to be busy—simply tell your visitor, politely but firmly, that you do not see sales reps without an appointment.

Why be so hard-nosed? First of all, a rep who succeeds at turning a surprise visit into a sales pitch is likely to try the same gambit again. Saying, "I'll visit with you this time but next time you'll need to have an appointment," is not very effective. It is much better for your rep to understand from the outset what your policy is and that you will stick to it. In this way, you will also establish a reputation for firmness that will stand you in good stead in your future interactions with the company.

When a sales rep is uncooperative on this score, you should not hesitate to contact her supervisor and complain. Consider the experience of this academic librarian:

> We had a sales rep from a major reference publisher who was particularly difficult to work with. He was always talking to us about his sales goals, and he always pitched his products very vigorously, even aggressively. I generally got the impression that he didn't know or care much

about the needs of my library or its patrons; he just wanted to sell the stuff he needed to sell in order to meet his own goals. I really didn't enjoy meeting with him at all. Once he called me and said that he was going to be in town visiting another customer and wanted to come by and see me. I told him, truthfully, that I was busy and did not have the time on that day. He showed up anyway, saying that he just wanted to give me some information about their upcoming new product line. When I saw him approaching my office, I stood up to demonstrate that I wasn't going to sit down and have a meeting with him. He walked in and remained standing as well, put a bunch of literature on the desk in front of me, and stood there talking for almost twenty minutes before I was finally able to get him out the door. That was the last straw; I called the vice president for sales at the publisher and told him I didn't want to see that rep again. They gave me a new rep, and things have been much better since.

This librarian did exactly the right thing. While it is important to be considerate and professional in your dealings with sales reps, it is also important to insist on the same behavior from them. Remember that for the most part, companies that sell to libraries are very concerned that your experiences with their representatives be positive, and they are generally only too happy to replace an unacceptable rep with one who is likely to give you better service.

11.3 AN EXCEPTION TO THE PUNCTUALITY RULE

There is one exception to the rule about punctuality, but while it is a useful one, it should be applied with caution.

In the business world—and make no mistake, when you are dealing with vendors the rules of the business world prevail—questions of relative power can be quite important. The fact that your sales rep comes to you, inviting you to buy a product and perhaps taking you out for a nice lunch in the process, implies that you wield a certain amount of power in that relationship (after all, you do not usually see librarians treating vendors to lunch or hopefully submitting formal proposals to purchase their products). Standing when someone enters a room is a way of ceding power to that person, and for that reason many businesspeople will choose to stand in a waiting room rather than sit; it keeps the power relationship more equal when the person for whom he or she is waiting appears.

Another very common way of asserting power in a relationship is, of course, to keep the other person waiting. It is a technique that can come in handy, as long as it is used judiciously. If the sales rep with whom you have an appointment is coming from a vendor or publisher that has been giving you problems and has not been sufficiently quick or thorough in fixing them, you can send a subtle message to your rep by making her wait a few minutes before you show up for your appointment. You want this person to feel a little bit like a supplicant, and you want to demonstrate that you are in control of the meeting.

Be careful: in matters such as these, subtle variations in approach can make a large difference. For example, if you arrive late to your appointment wearing your coat and carrying your bags from the car, you will send the wrong message entirely—not "I am in control" but rather "I am disorganized and unreliable." The same will be true if you arrive a half-hour late, rather than just a few minutes late. When your rep arrives, it should be clear that you are not there to greet her because other, more important matters have gotten in the way. The unspoken message is "I am aware of our appointment and will be here as soon as I can break away from dealing with the many issues and problems that require my attention. As a person of importance, there are many demands on my time."

If you decide to try this gambit, do not waste your time (and your sales rep's) by making her wait more than a few minutes. What matters is that she arrive first; you should appear no more than several minutes later. When you do arrive, apologize briefly for the delay (do not offer an explanation; explaining yourself implies that you need an excuse for keeping her waiting) and move briskly to the business at hand—which will probably be the changes that you expect this vendor to make in the way it does business with your library.

11.4 GOT PROBLEMS? GIVE SPECIFICS

If you are having problems with a vendor, be prepared to describe those problems accurately and to give specific examples when your rep arrives. Preparation will usually mean more than saying to yourself, "I've got to remember to talk about those shipping errors when our Acme rep comes tomorrow." It means actual preparation, and ideally it will mean having examples and documentation that your rep can take away with her after her visit.

UNHELPFUL	HELPFUL
"We keep getting books on approval that don't fit the profile."	"We've been getting books on approval that don't seem to fit our profile. Here are three recent examples; can you help me figure out why they came?"
"We've been having problems lately with incorrect entries on our invoices."	"Here are copies of several recent invoices that have had incorrect entries on them; you can see the incorrect entries highlighted in yellow. We're not sure why this keeps happening. Could you take these back and have someone look into it?"
"It takes you guys way too long to respond to problem calls."	"Over the past month we've called our customer service rep seven times with problems of one kind or another. It took him at least two days to get back to us on each one, and in one case we didn't hear from him for four days. These are the problems we called about, the dates we called and the dates the problems were finally resolved. We're very concerned about this."
"We never get our periodical issues on time"	"Over the past six months we've had to claim a lot more than we did this time last year, and more of them are going to second and third claims. Here's a spreadsheet showing the pattern. Can you tell us why we're seeing this new pattern of delays?

Three rules for working with sales reps:

- Insist on appointments, and make sure that you are punctual.
- Let your rep sell, and say no when you mean no.
- Provide detailed explanations of problems, and expect that the vendor's staff be able to understand and follow up on them appropriately.

Bear in mind that general statements are not usually very helpful to someone who is trying to find and correct process problems. Instead, provide concrete examples of problems that can be retraced and analyzed.

The problem with presenting this kind of detail to your sales rep is that it takes a lot of time and preparation beforehand. But the problem with only giving her general statements is that general statements give her nothing to work with. If she returns to headquarters and tells the staff there that "Crandall Public Library is getting the wrong books on approval," she has offered them no useful information. Unless they have examples of out-of-scope books that they can compare to the library's profile, they have no way of figuring out what the problem is. The same applies to the other examples above. The vendor has a responsibility to fix the problem, but the customer has an equally important responsibility to define the problem and to present it clearly so that a solution is possible.

11.5 LET HER SELL

Always bear in mind that a sales rep's job is not only to make sure that you are happy with the products and services you are currently getting, but also to inform you about new products and services and to encourage you to buy those that seem like a good match for your library's needs. Do not be offended when your rep inquires about your budget situation, or pitches a new service to you, or asks whether you are satisfied with the service you are getting from a competitor. If you are not the right person to answer such questions, say so clearly and politely and offer to refer your rep to the appropriate person. If you are not in a position to consider new products or services at the moment, again, simply say so clearly and politely. If your rep takes offense or disregards your wishes, look into getting a new rep.

11.6 LET YOUR NO BE NO

If it is clear to you that your response to a sales pitch is going to be "no," do not try to spare your sales rep's feelings by pretending that you will consider the matter further, or by asking for a demo or trial access, or by otherwise leading her on. If you are saying no because of what are hopefully temporary budget constraints, invite her to ask again later in the year (or next year). If you are saying no because the product is outside your library's collection scope, explain briefly why this is so. Consider these examples of polite, but firm, negative responses to sales pitches:

- "This does look like a quality product, but since we don't have a degree program in civil engineering, I couldn't justify spending this much money on it."
- "Due to a county budget shortfall, we've had to freeze all purchases over $1,000 for the rest of the fiscal year. But the outlook for next year is better, so remind me about this product when you come to visit next spring."
- "I like the content of this database, but the interface isn't very easy to use. I might be interested in a future release, but for now this isn't going to work for us."
- "We have all the ready-reference materials we need for this subject area right now."

Again, if your rep takes the rejection of her company's products personally or insists on pursuing the sale even after you have made clear that your answer is no, you should consider asking for a different rep.

11.7 INTERACTING WITH SALES REPS AT CONFERENCES

While you should expect to receive regular in-house visits from salespersons representing those vendors and publishers with whom you do a large amount of business each year, you will see many others personally only at conferences and meetings—and, of course, you will see many of your major reps at those meetings as well. Indeed, one significant reason for attending conferences and meetings is the opportunity that they offer to hold face-to-face meetings with many different vendor and publisher reps at one time. Some of these meetings will be brief and incidental, others will be pre-arranged and formal, and some will take the form of a shared lunch or dinner which may or may not involve a significant amount of business talk. Most of your interactions with reps will take place in the following venues:

- **At the vendor's booth.** Many conferences (though not all—see sidebar) will feature a large space set aside for vendors and publishers to display and promote their products. These products will include such obvious goods and services as books, approval plans, integrated library systems, subscription services and online databases; at larger meetings that draw a cross-section of librarians from many different kinds of libraries, you will also see very specialized vendors selling items like story-time props, buttons and T-shirts promoting the library profession, and ergonomic office furniture. If you spend much time attending professional meetings, you may find that some of your most valuable hours are spent not in the programmed sessions themselves, but in conversation with representatives of your vendors on the floor of the exhibit hall. Sometimes members of the vendor's executive management will be available at the booth as well, giving you what will often be your only chance to talk to senior decision-makers directly. Make the most of these opportunities by looking over the exhibitor list that comes with your conference program, seeing which vendors are going to be there, and making specific plans to visit with those with whom you need to talk. Other conferees will be vying for their time and attention as well, so have an idea of what you want to discuss before you get there—make your point and ask your questions quickly, and make follow-up appointments as needed.

Rule of Thumb: Exhibit halls are a great place to hear about upcoming products or releases, and a good place to give feedback on broad service or content issues. They are not a good place for long meetings.

- **Dinners or lunches.** If your job in the library includes making final decisions (or leading a group that makes final decisions) about whether to purchase a vendor's products or services, you can expect that at least some of those vendors will invite you out to lunch or dinner during the conference—either because they wish to cultivate you as a potential customer, or because they want to keep your business and take the opportunity to get your feedback. The larger your library's budget, the more likely it is that you will be cultivated as a prospect; similarly, the more business you do with a particular vendor, the more likely it is you will be invited out to dinner or lunch by that vendor. While the mood at these meals is usually informal and friendly, and the conversations will often focus on personal or general topics, the vendor rep may take the opportunity to talk about future developments and upcoming product releases, and you should take the opportunity to ask questions and make suggestions as well. Obviously, though, this would not be the place for serious criticisms of the company's services or products—especially if librarians from the vendor's other customer institutions are present.

WHY DOESN'T THIS MEETING HAVE VENDOR EXHIBITS?

When you attend a large meeting like the annual American Library Association conference or the annual meeting of a large state library association, the exhibit hall will be large, perhaps even overwhelming. You will find vendors of all kinds, offering everything from integrated library systems to children's books. And yet at some meetings, you will see no vendor exhibits at all. Why is that?

Several national meetings—notably the Charleston Conference, the Timberline Institute, and the annual meeting of the North American Serials Interest Group (NASIG)—are explicitly designed as events in which librarians, publishers and vendors can meet together to discuss industry issues and trends without any commercial pressure. At these meetings, vendors are expected to refrain from trying to sell their products, either formally (by means of exhibits and presentations) or informally (by means of product pitches in the hallway). The strictness of that limitation varies somewhat from meeting to meeting. On the one hand, organizers of the NASIG meeting are known for being very strict, even to the point of asking vendors not to invite librarians out for dinner during the meeting (most meals are included in the registration cost and eaten in a common area). On the other hand, the Charleston Conference has recently instituted a brief pre-conference "vendor showcase" to allow vendors to display their products and services before the official beginning of the conference program. Usually when you register for a meeting, conference information—available online or in printed packets—informs you as to what to expect from the vendors in attendance.

- **Focus groups.** Many vendors and publishers use conferences as an opportunity to gather small, representative groups of librarians together and get their opinions on current product offerings, possible future releases and general trends. Sometimes these meetings will be geared for a large audience, and the vendor will issue a general invitation (via an online discussion group or general mailing) asking anyone who is interested to attend. Other meetings will be smaller and more focused, and attendance will be by invitation only. You may be offered a stipend for attendance at these smaller meetings, or they may take place over a catered breakfast or lunch (see Chapter 17 for a discussion of the ethics of accepting such payments and enticements). Meetings such as these offer an excellent opportunity both to provide feedback to the company and to help shape its new and upcoming products or services.

11.8 BE ASSERTIVE BUT REASONABLE

In dealing with sales reps, the balance between assertiveness and reasonableness is extremely important, as has been noted in the different areas addressed above. That balance can be summarized as follows:

- Insist on appointments, and make sure that you are punctual.
- Let your rep sell, and say no when you mean no.
- Report problems promptly, and insist on their timely resolution.
- Provide detailed explanations of problems, and expect that the vendor's staff be able to understand and follow up on them appropriately.

Treat your rep as an equal partner in a business relationship, extending the same courtesy and professionalism to her as you would expect in return, and you will find that what can sometimes be a tense and adversarial relationship will instead be mutually helpful and enjoyable.

12 WORKING WITH CUSTOMER SERVICE REPRESENTATIVES

You and your staff will have regular interactions with sales representatives from your vendors and service providers, but for most library staff those interactions will not be very frequent. Your interactions with customer service representatives, however, will be both regular and frequent—sometimes taking place several times per week—and the quality of those interactions will make a tremendous difference in how smoothly and efficiently your staff is able to carry out its duties.

In Chapter 10 we discussed the importance of putting pleasant and competent people on the front lines of your interaction with vendors, and covered some specific "fire prevention" strategies. In this chapter we focus on the role of the customer service rep and some broader principles for making your work with them more enjoyable and productive.

12.1 YOU MAY NOT BE EQUALS, BUT YOU ARE BOTH CUSTOMERS

Wise corporate managers help their employees understand the concept of the "internal customer." According to this principle, employees recognize that the goods or services they produce—their "outputs," in management jargon—are used not only by the company's external customers, but also by those with whom they work inside the company. In libraries, this idea applies equally well: the acquisitions assistant who opens a box of books and organizes them on a cart is not only providing service to the patrons who need those books cataloged and delivered to the shelves, but also to the cataloger who will receive the books for processing. Similarly, the serials clerk who puts a note in an order record does so with the ultimate intent of making materials available to patrons but also with the short-term intent of keeping colleagues in the department aware of the order's status. These dual realities imply the need for a balanced perspective: Everyone who works in the library should keep the ultimate needs of patrons in mind when performing tasks and designing work flows, but all should also consider the more immediate needs of those colleagues who will be receiving and further processing their own outputs.

12.2 TREAT THE VENDOR AS AN "INTERNAL" CUSTOMER

The relationship of library staff to patrons is simple: the library staff is there to serve; patrons are the reason the library has a staff. The relationship of library staff to each other is fairly simple, as well: members of the library staff are colleagues, and should be professionally considerate of each other and willing to make adjustments in practices and work flow so that the ordering and processing of materials is efficient and effective. But the relationship between library staff and a vendor's customer-service staff is more complicated. On the one hand, the library staff has a traditional vendor-customer relationship with your service providers and should expect to be treated as a customer. On the other hand, the vendor must receive and process "outputs" from the library staff, and should expect reasonable treatment as well.

What are the outputs that a library sends to a vendor, and which it should (within reason) shape to fit the vendor's needs? Most are fairly obvious, and so are the ways in which library staff can reasonably be expected to conform to the vendor's expectations:

- **Purchase orders** should be formatted in a way that is clear to the vendor, and submitted according to mutually-agreed processes;
- **Claims** should be easily distinguishable from purchase orders, and submitted according to mutually-agreed processes and schedules;
- **Invoice payments** should be promptly and correctly rendered;
- **Returns** should be sent only according to mutually-agreed schedules and criteria.

Other outputs are less concrete, and more subtle—phone calls, for example. It is your customer service rep's job to answer your call pleasantly and professionally and to respond to your needs quickly and competently. On the other hand, it is the library staffer's job to know whom he should call with a particular type of problem, to present the problem clearly and accurately, and to work with the customer service rep in a pleasant and professional manner.

> **Rule of Thumb:** Think of such things as your orders, claims, and phone calls, as "outputs"and your vendor as the "customer" for those outputs.

12.3 MAKE IT EASY FOR THE VENDOR TO SERVE YOU WELL

Taking carefully into account the effect of your practices on the vendor—in other words, thinking of the vendor as a sort of "internal customer" for your staff's outputs—does not necessarily mean bending over backwards to accommodate the vendor's every preference. You will sometimes have to say no to a vendor's request, the same way you sometimes have to say no to a patron. It does, however, mean making a good-faith effort to submit your outputs to the vendor in a way that works well for the vendor's staff and workflows.

A reasonable question here, of course, is why. Why on earth should the customer feel obliged to adapt to the needs of its vendors and service providers? The answer is that, beyond the basic legal and ethical requirements of doing business in the marketplace (which demand, for example, that you pay your invoices on time) your library really is not under such an obligation. You can feel free to insist that all of your vendors adapt to you, and your vendors can then decide whether the cost of adapting to your preference is worth the benefit of doing business with you. Make no mistake, some vendors will choose not to do business with you if you adopt such an approach, but most of them will swallow hard and do what you ask. The problem then is that you are making it more difficult for your vendor to give you good service, and that is never a wise course of action. While you should expect the vendor's staff to work hard to give you good service, it is also in your best interest to do what you can to make it as easy for them to do so as possible.

Consider the following hypothetical exchange between a library staffer and a subscription agent:

> **Library:** Hello, I need to talk to someone about an outstanding claim.
>
> **Vendor:** I'm sorry, are you calling about an invoice we haven't paid?
>
> **Library:** No, I'm calling because it's May and we're still waiting for the November issue of one of our journals.
>
> **Vendor:** Oh, I see—you're looking for someone in our subscriptions area. This is the reception desk.
>
> **Library:** Yes, I need our customer service rep.
>
> **Vendor:** Do you know his or her name?
>
> **Library:** It's Tina something, I think.
>
> **Vendor:** Just a moment and I'll transfer you.

Tina Kingsley: Customer service, this is Tina Kingsley; may I help you?

Library: This is Ted from Brenner University. We've been claiming the November issue of the Journal of Cytophysiology for several months now, and still haven't received it. Can you tell me what's going on?

Vendor: Brenner University? I think you need Tina Carlsson—she's the rep for your region. I'm Tina *Kingsley*: I work with overseas customers. Hang on just a moment and I'll transfer you.

Tina Carlsson: Tina Carlsson, may I help you?

Library: This is Ted from Brenner University. We've been claiming the November issue of the Journal of Cytophysiology for several months now, and still haven't received it. Can you tell me what's going on?

Tina Carlsson: Let me look that up for you. Hmmm, it doesn't look like we have your subscription on record. Actually, I don't see that title in our system at all. Do you have an ISSN?

Library: 7723-8155.

Tina Carlsson: Oh, I see the problem; that ISSN is for Advances in Cytophysiology.

Library: That's right, it's Advances in Cytophysiology. Sorry.

Tina Carlsson: My records indicate that we sent out your missing issue about three weeks ago—it definitely should have arrived by now. If it hasn't, though, I'll be sure to send you another one. Could you double-check for me and make sure it isn't there?

Library: Actually, the receiving shelves are near my desk—let me go look. (Pause) You're right, it was there all along. Sorry to bother you!

In this example, the library staffer was creating an "output" for the vendor to use. That output was a telephone claim. A telephone claim is a perfectly legitimate output, of course, and the vendor's job in a situation like this is to respond to it quickly and effectively. But in order for the vendor to do so, the library must take care to do a few things right, and unless it does so it will probably be difficult for the vendor to deliver the expected service.

Consider the example above. One thing that any library staffer really ought to know before picking up the phone to call a vendor is the phone number that will actually lead him to the appropriate contact person. Knowing the contact person's full name is also a very good idea. If the staffer is calling about a subscription or a book, he ought to be sure he knows the title in question. Above all, if he is calling to take a vendor to task for unresponsiveness, he should double-check before calling to make sure that the vendor has not actually responded since he last contacted them.

Usually, as in the example above, the staffer's confusion can be cleared up in the course of a single phone call. Sometimes, though, a bad library output can lead the vendor on a fruitless search for a nonexistent item or create confusion at the vendor's end that slows down the resolution process and creates unnecessary work for all involved. The better you and your staff prepare before contacting a vendor, the easier it will be for your vendor to give you the service you expect.

12.4 BE ASSERTIVE BUT REASONABLE

In Chapter 11 we discussed the necessity of being willing to ask for a new sales rep if your current rep's behavior or business practices are less than professional, or if she is simply not meeting the needs of your library. The same is true of customer service reps; there is a certain level of effectiveness and professionalism that you should expect, and if that expectation is consistently not being met, you should notify his or her supervisor and request that someone else be put in charge of your account. Examples of reasonable service standards include:

- **Timely responses to calls and messages.** If you call and leave a message with your customer service rep, or if you send her an e-mail message alerting her to a problem you are experiencing with the vendor's services, you should get a return call or e-mail message within twenty-four hours at the very latest—if your message was left or sent early in the business day, you ought to get a response by the end of that day. This is not the same thing as insisting that the problem itself be solved within twenty-four hours; obviously, that will not always be possible. But if it is going to take longer than one business day to fix the problem, your rep should respond within that time frame to let you know that your message has been received, to tell you what is being done to solve the problem, and to give you at least a tentative idea of when the problem will be solved.

- **Professional demeanor.** In Chapter 10 we discussed the importance of training your library staff not to assume treachery on the part of vendors where an honest error is more likely to blame. Staffers who approach their reps with suspicion and mistrust are not likely to work very effectively with those reps.

Reasonable expectations for customer service reps:

- Timely responses to calls and e-mail messages
- Professional demeanor
- Knowledge of the vendor's services and systems
- Familiarity with the customer's organization and needs
- Reasonable workload

Similarly, library staff should expect that a vendor's customer service rep will not respond defensively or angrily when told about a problem or error on the vendor's side. Rudeness, condescension, impatience and sarcasm are never acceptable, and a library staffer who experiences those behaviors when dealing with a customer service rep should notify his supervisor in the library immediately. The supervisor should take quick steps to ensure that those behaviors are not repeated— either by insisting on a new rep, or (in cases where the unprofessional behavior was mild or unusual) by seeing to it that the offending rep is warned.

- **Knowledge of the vendor's services and systems.** It goes without saying that a customer service rep needs to be intimately familiar with the services, processes, and systems of the vendor for which he works. Yet such is not always the case. In your dealings with each of your vendors, watch for indications that brand-new hires are being put on the phone without adequate training. Where you see indications of such practices, question them and insist on better preparation for your reps, especially if the vendor is one to which you are paying substantial service fees. Remember that while you should be willing to make an effort to keep things going smoothly between you and your vendors, you should not allow your vendors to use you and your staff as adjunct trainers for their employees. It is the vendor's job to put knowledgeable and well-trained people on the front lines of customer service; it is not the customers' job to provide knowledge and training to vendors' employees.

- **Familiarity with the customer's organization and needs.** Beyond general knowledge of and competence in the services, practices, and systems of the vendor for which she works, a customer service rep must also have some familiarity with the particular array of services her employer provides to each of the customers for which she is responsible. She should know the names of her primary contacts, and have some knowledge of the nature and specific needs of the institutions themselves. Few customer service reps will be able to carry all of the relevant information in their heads, but it is easy enough to keep a binder or computer file handy, filled with basic information about each customer.

Rule of Thumb: *A vendor that aggressively pursues new customers without proportionately increasing its staff will provide progressively worse service to its customers.*

• **Reasonable workload.** It follows from the above requirement that you should expect your library vendor to maintain a staff large enough to provide an acceptable level of service to all of its customers. Beware the vendor that brags about its ever-expanding business, but responds evasively to questions about how or whether it is expanding its service staff in order to provide service to all of its new customers. Members of your staff should keep their eyes and ears open to hints that the customer service reps with whom they work are overextended. If you get the impression that such is the case, mention it to your sales rep. Suggest that your library will not want to add any additional services or expand the scope of the ones it currently gets unless it is sure that the vendor is prepared to fully support the services it already provides.

12.5 LET MERCY TEMPER JUSTICE

While you should insist that the vendor meet reasonable standards such as those above, you should also bear in mind that the best vendors (and their representatives) have better and worse days and are sometimes impacted by forces over which they have no control. Do not be too quick to bring down a supervisor's wrath on the head of an employee who has offended.

13 TRACKING VENDOR PERFORMANCE

In the last chapter, we discussed the importance of insisting that your vendors and service providers be responsive to your needs when problems and questions arise. But it is worth pointing out that an important part of your vendor's job is to keep those problems and questions to a minimum in the first place. In addition to making sure you get timely and helpful responses to your specific inquiries, you should also be keeping an eye on your vendors' general, day-to-day accuracy and effectiveness.

13.1 FULFILLMENT RATES

Fulfillment—or, in other words, how successful a vendor is at getting you the items you order quickly and accurately—is one of the most basic criteria against which libraries judge vendors. Fulfillment can be measured in three dimensions:

- **Timeliness:** How quickly is the order fulfilled?
- **Accuracy:** Did you get the exact item you ordered?
- **Completeness:** Did you get *all* the items you ordered?

Libraries' ability to track fulfillment locally will vary somewhat depending on the capabilities of their integrated systems; however, most book vendors can generate their own fulfillment reports and those reports should be among those that your sales rep brings during her regular visits. (Ideally, your book vendor's Web site should also offer you the option of running fulfillment analyses whenever you wish.)

In the serials realm, where the vendor responds to an order by instituting an ongoing process of delivery rather than by simply sending you a single item, analyzing fulfillment can be a bit more complicated. In a serials context, the issues are still timeliness, completeness, and accuracy, but you will judge the vendor's performance in those areas by asking yourself questions like these:

- Does my vendor supply new issues promptly upon publication? (Timeliness)

> Three dimensions of fulfillment:
>
> - Timeliness: How quickly is the order fulfilled?
> - Accuracy: Did you get the exact item you ordered?
> - Completeness: Did you get *all* the items you ordered?

- Does my vendor consistently supply all the issues to which I am entitled, or are there gaps in coverage? (Completeness)

- Do I get the subscriptions I order, or does my vendor sometimes institute subscriptions for the wrong titles? (Accuracy)

Of course, another complicating factor when working with serials vendors is the fact that the subscription agent is somewhat at the mercy of the journal or magazine publisher, so delays and gaps in coverage will not necessarily be the agent's fault.

When you are considering establishing a relationship with a new serials vendor or are comparing data for the purpose of choosing between two vendors, make sure you ask several of that vendor's existing customers about fulfillment—and in doing so, do not limit yourself to references provided by the vendor.

FULFILLMENT RATES: COMPARING APPLES TO APPLES

Most libraries tend to concentrate their book orders with one or two vendors, but some spread their ordering activity out more broadly. If you need to compare fulfillment rates between two or more different vendors, make sure you are comparing apples to apples. Librarians usually use different vendors because those vendors have different strengths—one vendor may be good at getting newly published books to your library promptly, whereas another may be a better source for older and out-of-print titles. Obviously, to hold both vendors to the same standard of timeliness would not be reasonable; the vendor that is valued for its ability to track down and deliver out-of-print books will score lower on timeliness than the one with a reputation for speedy delivery of new books. On the other hand, both vendors should be held to the same standards of accuracy. There will not usually be any need for complicated statistical formulas or painstaking quantification when making these comparisons—keep in mind the different types of service you expect from each vendor, and let common sense guide you in your interpretation of the fulfillment data you collect.

13.2 CLAIM RESPONSES

No matter how good your book vendor or subscription agent, there will be times when the fulfillment of an order is delayed and you must issue a claim. A claim is a message from your library to the vendor that says, in essence, "Where's the stuff we ordered?" (In the case of a prepaid item or a subscription, the message is a bit more insistent: "Where's the stuff we paid for?") Claims arise from different circumstances depending on the nature of the original order, but they are all variations on that basic theme. The three basic variations are these:

- **Serials claims:** "We should have received issue X by this point; where is it?"
- **Firm-order claims:** "We ordered this book two months ago; where is it?"
- **Approval claims:** "Shouldn't we have received this book on approval?"

When it comes to claiming, you will evaluate your vendors based on two basic factors: whether you are having to claim more often than you should, and how well the vendor responds to your claims.

13.3 HOW FREQUENTLY DO YOU HAVE TO CLAIM?

This is an issue that can cause some friction between vendors and libraries, because there are librarians who claim too frequently and there are vendors who respond too slowly. For most libraries with integrated systems, claiming periods are established ahead of time and claims are generated automatically by the system. A common rule is for a first claim to be submitted either forty-five days after the missing issue's expected date or halfway between the current issue's expected date and the expected date of the next one, whichever comes first. Appropriate claiming periods for firm orders will vary widely, depending on the nature of the title on order. If the title is a foreign publication, or a scholarly title originally published more than a year prior to the order, you should give your vendor more leeway than if it is a recent, domestically-published trade book. In general, it is reasonable

Rule of Thumb: The basic unit of time in a claiming period is usually one month; claims are usually submitted after thirty days, forty-five days, or sixty days.

to claim books that fall into the latter category if they have not arrived within thirty to forty-five days of your order. Vendors should be able to expect the same reasonableness from you in your claiming that you expect from them in their invoicing. If you are dealing with an irregularly-published journal from a small society publisher, for example, try not to pepper the company with claims every two weeks between issues. In claiming, even more than in many other areas of acquisitions and serials work, it is essential that you maintain a balance between assertiveness and reasonableness.

Claims on approval are not quite the same thing as serial or firm-order claims. In the case of a subscription, a standing order or a firm order, you are asking the vendor to explain why it has not sent an item you specifically requested. In the case of a claim on approval, you are asking why a book that you believe should have been a good match for your library's profile was not sent. (You also may be asking that a specific book be included with your approval books, regardless of whether or not it fits your profile.) These claims are obviously handled as they arise, and if they follow a clear pattern, they may lead you to make adjustments to your profile.

13.4 HOW WELL DOES THE VENDOR RESPOND TO CLAIMS?

You will need to evaluate your vendors not only on how often it is necessary to submit claims to them, but also on how helpful and effective they are in receiving and responding to your claims. Ask yourself the following questions:

> Evaluating a vendor's responsiveness to claims
>
> • Does the vendor make it easy for me to claim?
> • Is the vendor's staff knowledgeable and responsive?
> • How soon does the vendor respond to claims?
> • How soon do I get the item I have claimed?
> • Does the vendor keep me informed, or do I have to ask repeatedly for status reports?

- Does the vendor give me an easy way to submit claims, or does it seem deliberately to make that process difficult?
- When I talk with a person about a claim, does that person know what I am talking about and seem genuinely engaged in fixing the problem?
- When I submit a claim, how soon do I get a response?
- When I submit a claim, how soon do I get the item I am claiming?
- Does the vendor keep me informed about the status of my claim, or do I have to call back repeatedly to get updated information?

Obviously, the best vendor is one that functions so efficiently that you rarely need to claim, and on those rare occasions that you must claim, makes the process easy by automatically placing the desired item on backorder and keeping you informed of its progress in fulfilling the order. But it should be equally obvious that these processes will fail occasionally with even the best vendor, either because of human error or because of failings on the part of the publisher. As in all areas of serials and acquisitions work, it is important to balance a firm expectation of good service with a pragmatic recognition that no vendor will provide perfect service all the time.

13.5 ANALYZING THE QUALITY OF CUSTOMER SERVICE

In Chapter 12 we discussed the importance of holding your customer service representatives firmly to reasonable standards of service quality. One important part of doing so is to maintain an accurate record of problems you experience with your representatives, as well as examples of any truly heroic service the rep has provided. Such information will come in handy when your sales rep comes to visit, or when you are considering switching vendors. It is tempting to think that your front-line staff, some of whom will be deeply familiar with the performance of your vendors' customer-service staff, will be able to give off-the-cuff assessments of service quality as needed, but bear in mind that staff sometimes leave. Information that may be needed in the future should reside in places more permanent and reliable than the brains of librarians and their staff. Keep a file devoted to service quality for each vendor, either in paper or electronically, and use it to record bad experiences, good experiences and, especially, patterns of service quality. Does the vendor tend to do well in certain situations and badly in others? Do you regularly run into trouble with one member of the vendor's staff, but not with others? Keep track of any such patterns, and address them as necessary with your sales rep when she comes to visit.

Rule of Thumb: Keep a record of noteworthy interactions with your vendors—both positive and negative.

13.6 ANALYZING INVOICING PRACTICES

Invoicing is one of your vendor's most basic and important customer service functions. Inaccurate or difficult-to-interpret invoices, or those sent too early or too late, cause confusion—and "confusion" and

A good invoice:

- Is printed clearly and legibly;
- Is clearly identified as an invoice;
- Is clearly distinct from a credit memo;
- Clearly lists the items for which you are being charged, and the price for each;
- Allows you some flexibility in the way processing charges are calculated and displayed.

"invoice" are two words that you never want to see used in the same sentence.

When you are considering doing business with a vendor for the first time, you should ask to see examples of the vendor's invoices. You should also ask to see an example of its credit memos, which notify you when a credit is applied to your account. Evaluate the invoices based on the following criteria:

- Are they printed clearly and legibly?
- Are they clearly identified as invoices?
- Do the vendor's credit memos look confusingly similar to its invoices?
- Are the items for which you are being charged clearly labeled?
- Can you choose how processing charges are calculated and displayed?

Again, the primary criterion when judging invoices is **clarity**. There should be no ambiguity whatsoever as to the function of that slip of paper, what you are being charged for, how much you are being charged for it, or how much you owe in total. In Chapter 15 we discuss methods of recognizing and dealing with scam vendors, and we will return to this point; the artfully ambiguous invoice is one of the main weapons in a scammer's arsenal, and being alert to such invoices is your first line of defense against such vendors.

13.7 ANALYZING COVERAGE

Another important criterion to apply when evaluating vendor performance is coverage. This term refers simply to a vendor's ability to get all the things you would like to order. A vendor may claim to offer "worldwide coverage," or may specialize in publications from a particular geographical area—there are, for example, vendors that specialize in Canadian books or in publications from the United Kingdom. A vendor may also specialize in particular types of publication—out-of-print books, textbooks, periodicals, reference books. Before you begin doing business with a vendor, you should establish clearly what sort of coverage the vendor is offering; do not expect a vendor that specializes in quick provision of newly-published scholarly books to excel in out-of-print services unless that vendor claims to be strong in both areas.

Telltale signs of insufficient coverage:

- Faculty members in a particular area seem to call regularly to ask why a book has not yet arrived.
- You are seeing books in stores long before they arrive in your library, despite the fact that you placed orders for them well in advance of their publication dates.
- You are having to send claims repeatedly for books of a certain type or from a certain publisher.

Once you have established the relationship, actually monitoring your vendor's performance in terms of coverage is not always easy or straightforward, because the only way to detect a problem in coverage is to know what you are not receiving. However, there are telltale signs for which you can watch, all of which can alert you to a possible problem:

- Faculty members in a particular area seem to call regularly to ask why a book has not yet arrived.
- You are seeing books in stores long before they arrive in your library, despite the fact that you placed orders for them well in advance of their publication dates.
- You are having to send claims repeatedly for books of a certain type or from a certain publisher.

Bear in mind that coverage problems do not necessarily mean that you should stop doing business with a particular vendor. They may mean, however, that you should consider sending orders of a particular type to a different vendor, one that specializes in that specific type of publication. Of course, the law of diminishing returns applies here—if you establish too many different ordering channels for too many different kinds of publication, you may end up paying a high price in staff time and effort to achieve a relatively small improvement in service quality. The best approach is to think in fairly broad terms: find vendors who are especially good at covering new publications, out-of-print books, foreign publications, standing orders and serials, and then refine your approach as necessary from there.

13.8 TECHNICAL PROCESSING

Many libraries pay their vendors extra to process physically the books or serials they provide. Such processing services may range from the very basic (providing brief cataloging records, for example) to the comprehensive (full cataloging and physical processing of books, down to the library's property stamp and security strip). If your library is going to want such services, you will obviously need to assess before you start to do business with a vendor whether the scope of the services it offers is a good match for your library's needs. This may not be simply a question of whether a particular service appears on the menu; it is also a question of whether the vendor will provide the service in a manner that fits well with your local systems.

Once you resolve these questions and establish the relationship, you will need to monitor your vendor's processing services and judge them according to two criteria:

- Whether the vendor is doing what it said it would;
- Whether the vendor is performing those tasks accurately and well.

As for the first of those criteria, the questions you ask yourself might include the following:

- Is the vendor including the correct type of security device, in the place you specified?
- Are the barcodes in the position they should be?
- Do the spine labels include the information you agreed upon?
- Is the vendor applying the type of jacket cover agreed upon?
- Are the catalog records complete?

As for the second criterion, you should ask yourselves questions such as these:

- Is the security device placed carefully and well?
- Do the barcodes on the books match those in the corresponding records?
- Are the spine labels printed clearly and durably?
- Are the jacket covers applied skillfully and carefully?
- Are the catalog records accurate?

Again, notice the difference between these two criteria: the first addresses whether the vendor is doing what it said it would, and the second addresses whether the vendor is doing the work well. These are equally important criteria, but a failing in one of them will call for a different sort of resolution than a failing in the other. If your books are showing up without spine labels despite the fact that you are paying for spine labels, the follow-up should be easy and straightforward. You call the vendor and ask why you are not getting spine labels, everyone consults their records and the necessary adjustments are made. If, however, you find that your spine labels are blurry or the ink is flaking off of them within three weeks of receipt, the follow-up and resolution process will be a bit more complicated and may involve competing perceptions ("I can read those spine labels just fine!"). If you do a considerable amount of business with the vendor in question, you may be able to insist that the vendor make adjustments in its processes and work flows to accommodate your local needs. But in some cases you may have to suspend the processing of your library's materials until the vendor can update its equipment, change suppliers, or reshuffle local staff. In this as in all other things, remember to maintain a healthy balance between assertiveness and reasonableness.

FURTHER READING:

Born, Kathleen. "Strategies for Selecting Vendors and Evaluating Their Performance—From the Vendor's Perspective." *Journal of Library Administration* 16 (1992), 111.

Maxwell, Kim, and Bob Boissy. "The Art of Claiming." *Serials Librarian* 42 (2002), 229. (This is a report of a workshop, rather than a formal article, but it includes quite a bit of useful information.)

IV. ENDING (OR AVOIDING) THE LIBRARY-VENDOR RELATIONSHIP

14 SWITCHING VENDORS

Like most relationships, the ones between your library and its various vendors will have ups and downs. Most of the "down" periods will occur as you are trying to work through problems, and most of the time you will succeed and things will get better. But not always, and sometimes the problems you cannot work out will be serious enough to make you decide to stop doing business with a vendor.

In the great majority of cases, this will mean transferring your business from one vendor to another, since the vendor you are dropping is, presumably, serving one of your library's ongoing needs. In this chapter we discuss good and bad reasons for dropping a vendor, some general information about managing the change from one vendor to another, and tips for ending the relationship without making it impossible to reestablish one later if appropriate.

14.1 BAD REASONS FOR DROPPING A VENDOR

Ending a relationship with a vendor can be traumatic, sometimes surprisingly so. From an organizational standpoint, the implications can be fairly serious—you and your staff may need to learn how to use an entirely new online ordering database; you may have to define a new set of physical processing requirements; you will likely have to adjust to new shipping schedules; you will have to get to know a new array of contacts, and so forth. Then there is the emotional impact, which a good manager will not underestimate. If your library has been doing business with the vendor in question for a long time, and if your staff has been in place for a long time as well, there are likely to be interpersonal relationships that will be severed when you end the business relationship. The prospect of learning a new system, getting to know new representatives and contact people, and adjusting to new schedules and work flows can be daunting (and even depressing) to staff members who have grown comfortable with a long-established relationship. Do not be fooled into thinking that such considerations are trivial; when you solicit staff input on the issue of dropping a vendor, issues such as these will color their responses.

On the other hand, while these considerations should be dealt with sensitively, they should not drive the decision-making process. Bear in mind that your library exists to serve its patrons and its sponsoring institution, and that some degree of occasional stress or discomfort is par for the course in any job. As a library professional, your duty is to organize your work (and that of your staff) in the way that is ultimately of most benefit to the patron. But the above considerations do make it all the more essential that you approach the cessation of a vendor relationship carefully and thoughtfully before making a final decision. Above all, be certain that you are not considering this course of action for the wrong reasons. Bad reasons for dropping a vendor include the following:

> *Rule of Thumb: No good vendor will promise more than it can deliver. If a promise sounds to good to be true, it is probably an empty one.*

1. **Occasional service problems.** No vendor will provide perfect service. In fact, when investigating potential vendors, you should be especially on guard for those that make promises that sound too good to be true. No one will give you 100 percent fulfillment; no one can promise perfectly error-free invoicing, an unwavering shipment schedule, or unfailingly helpful reps. Even a significant vendor error, one which has caused considerable consternation or inconvenience for your library, should not be considered grounds for dropping the vendor if it is an isolated incident—unless, of course, criminal or unethical behavior was involved. Making one mistake, even one big mistake, is easy, and no amount of jumping from vendor to vendor will eliminate the risk of having to deal with such mistakes.

2. **Problems that are not the vendor's fault.** Remember that book jobbers and subscription agents are middlemen, not the ultimate suppliers of the materials you purchase from them. If a publisher delays a book's release, or if a scholarly journal skips an issue or publishes issues out of order, or if all of the shipping companies on the east coast go on strike in the same week, there is no point in yelling at your vendor. The vendor's response to such problems is, of course, within its control, and you should examine its response critically: does the vendor look for alternate shipping methods so that your shipment will be delayed as little as possible, or call the journal's publisher to find out when the missing issue is planned for publication, or find out the new release date for the book you ordered? The original problem may

Bad reasons for dropping a vendor:

- Occasional service problems
- Problems that are not the vendor's fault
- Problems that are your own fault
- The "grass is greener" syndrome

Rule of Thumb: You will never switch from an imperfect vendor to a perfect one; you will only trade one set of strengths and weaknesses for another.

have been outside the vendor's control, but it should do whatever it reasonably can to minimize the effects of that problem on its customers.

3. **Problems that are your own fault.** Before you abandon a vendor take a close look within your library. Why do the books you are receiving on approval not fit the scope of your collection? Why do your shipments always arrive on Friday—driving your staff crazy? Why do the compact discs your vendor supplies always contain recordings of the right work but the wrong performance? Why does the vendor's online ordering database not work the way it should? It is a mistake to point the finger until you make sure that the problems you are seeing really originate with the vendor, rather than with you or your staff. Have you taken the time to learn the ins-and-outs of how to use the vendor's online database? (It may be that its limitations are more a reflection of ignorance at your end than of weakness or poor design at the vendor's.) Is your ordering staff providing full discographical information with its compact disc orders? (Different recordings can be notoriously similar to each other in their details.) Did your predecessor in the position specifically request Friday delivery? How long has it been since you reviewed your approval profile? Remember that all of your vendors receive outputs from your library that affect their ability to serve you well, and poor library outputs will sabotage your vendors' best efforts.

4. **The "grass is greener" syndrome.** There are differences between vendors. Most have areas in which they excel and others do not, and depending on your needs, the size of your staff and your areas of collection focus, it can make a very big difference who your subscription agent or approval vendor is. However, you should bear in mind that when you leave one vendor for another, you will almost invariably trade one type of problem for another. Do your homework before switching and make sure that the new vendor's weaknesses are going to be less of an issue for you than the old one's were. You should also bear in mind that some problems simply come with the territory, and changing vendors is not likely to make a significant difference in those areas.

14.2 GOOD REASONS FOR CHANGING VENDORS

While it is important not to be too quick to drop a vendor or to do so for the wrong reasons, there are, of course, good reasons to do so—and, sometimes, to do so immediately. These include:

1. **Criminal or unethical behavior.** Every vendor makes mistakes, and it is wise to be, within reason, forgiving of mistakes that are unusual and that are clearly made in good faith. However, mistakes that are made in bad faith—in other words, errors that are deliberate and that are designed to defraud or cheat your library—must be regarded as grounds for the immediate cessation of your business relationship, and may be grounds for legal action as well. Such "errors" might include:

   a) Selling your library pirated materials, or materials which the vendor is otherwise unauthorized to redistribute;

   b) Sending invoices with inflated, hidden or specious charges;

   c) Offering you false, misleading or illegally-obtained information about a competitor;

   d) Attempting to bribe you or your staff;

   e) Sending you materials that you did not order, and then demanding payment (more on this topic in the next chapter).

   It is worth pointing out here that the difference between criminal and innocent mistakes can be difficult to discern—what may look at first like an intentionally doctored invoice is more likely to be an innocent error, if it comes from a vendor you know and trust. However, if there is any question about the nature of the error, you must place the burden of proof on the vendor's shoulders and may want to suspend doing business with that vendor until you are satisfied that the vendor is dealing with you in good faith.

2. **Patterns of bad service that do not change despite repeated efforts.** Again, every vendor will drop the

Rule of Thumb: It is always easier to start doing business again with a vendor you have temporarily suspended than it is to get your money back from a crooked one.

ball from time to time, and the librarian who jumps promiscuously from vendor to vendor in search of perfect fulfillment, flawless status reporting, and universal coverage, will eventually retire exhausted and embittered. However, there is a considerable difference between the occasional problems that arise in any library-vendor relationship and problems that are part of a recurring pattern that the vendor does not seem able (or willing) to correct. Ongoing problems fall into one of two categories:

a) **Those the vendor is not capable of fixing.** These are problems that may have to do with the vendor's physical location, its size, the nature of the marketplace, etc. When faced with ongoing problems that the vendor is incapable of fixing, you must ask yourself whether a) the problem is consequential enough to merit dropping the vendor, and b) whether the problem will actually be solved by going to another vendor. For example, consider the following hypothetical situation:

> The Brenner University Library has been given a mandate by the University administration to reduce the amount of paper waste it produces. Library management has determined that one very effective way of doing that would be to submit orders and claims electronically wherever possible. Acme Books, its primary vendor, offers an online ordering and collection management system, but the system is clunky and difficult to use, and the system is frequently down. Repeated requests for upgrades and improvements have been met with promises to fix the system, but no substantive changes have been forthcoming. After a year of badgering from the library, Acme finally confesses that it simply cannot afford to hire the people it would need to make its online system substantially better. Peerless Book Services, one of Acme's direct competitors, offers a much more functional online system.

> Assuming that in other significant regards, Peerless and Acme offer service of roughly the same

quality, the library in the above scenario has a powerful incentive to switch vendors: it has been given a mandate by its host institution to move its processes online, and its primary vendor is not capable of meeting the library's needs in this area.

b) **Those the vendor is unwilling to fix.** Sometimes the problem is not that the vendor is incapable of fixing the error you have been wrestling with—it is simply unwilling to do so. It is worth pointing out here that such a stance is not necessarily unreasonable. If your library is doing $25,000 worth of business annually with a subscription agent, the problem you are having is unique to your library, and the agent would not be able to fix your problem without investing $500,000 in infrastructure enhancements, the vendor must weigh the costs and benefits of making that investment and will probably decide to risk losing your business rather than spend an amount of money that is out of proportion to the benefit it will derive from doing so. (Librarians think this way, too, when they select a vendor based on the vendor's apparent ability to give the library the most value for its budget dollar.)

However, whether the vendor is being reasonable or unreasonable in its unwillingness to fix a problem, the questions you must ask yourself are the same as the ones you should ask when faced with a vendor that is unable to fix the problem: is the issue important enough to switch vendors, and can another vendor do better? If the answer to both questions is yes, then your course is clear.

3. **Changes in policy or practice that make the vendor a bad fit for your library.** Has your vendor recently stopped doing business with a publisher whose books or journals are central to your institution's research needs? Has it switched shippers from one that gave consistently good service to one that you have found to be incompetent or unreliable? If your vendor has actually made a conscious change in its policies or practices and those changes are going to mean a significant gap between its services and

Good reasons for dropping a vendor:

- Criminal or unethical behavior
- Patterns of bad service that do not change despite repeated efforts
- Changes in the vendor's policies or practices that make the vendor a bad fit for your library's needs
- Chronic unresponsiveness
- Chronic fiscal problems

your needs, you should consider taking your business elsewhere.

4. **Chronic unresponsiveness.** This is not quite the same thing as an inability or unwillingness to fix problems. Unresponsiveness is an unwillingness or inability even to respond appropriately to calls and requests. If you find that one of your vendors rarely (or never) returns your calls or e-mails, or that your calls are handed off to people who do not know how to address them, and if your attempts to take your concerns higher in the vendor's management structure are met with stonewalling or further unresponsiveness, then you should seriously consider ceasing to do business with that vendor.

5. **Chronic fiscal problems.** Pay attention to the fiscal health of your vendors. Keeping an eye on the professional literature and conversations in relevant online discussion groups will give you an idea of who is doing well and who is in trouble. While you should be careful not to jump to conclusions based on incomplete or potentially slanted information, you should begin asking questions and doing research about your vendor as soon as you begin hearing hints of fiscal trouble. Ask your sales rep direct questions, and be highly suspicious of less-than-direct answers.

Unfortunately, you will not always have the option of ceasing to do business with a vendor that provides unacceptably low levels of service. It is an unfortunate reality of library work that some vendors offer unique products or services that may be essential to your library's users, and in those cases you may be stuck dealing with subpar service. But this is not usually the case; in most cases, you can honestly threaten to take your business away from a vendor, and in most cases, that threat will get results.

14.3 MANAGING THE SWITCH

Depending on the vendors and the type of service involved, switching from one vendor to another may be a significant chore, or it may be a relatively easy matter of simply redirecting future orders.

To understand the difference between changing firm-order vendors and changing approval vendors or subscription agents, picture yourself standing in front of a row of barrels with a handful of pebbles. Suppose you have been throwing pebbles into one of those barrels all day, and you decide that you want to start throwing them into a different barrel. So you turn slightly and start aiming for another barrel. The analogy is a bit simplistic, of course, but that is basically what changing firm-order vendors is like: you stop sending orders to the old vendor and begin sending orders to the new one. It is relatively easy to switch because firm orders are separate and individual. Orders are not fulfilled immediately, of course, which does present some complication. You may decide to cancel all open orders with the old vendor and transfer them to the new one, or you may choose to leave previously-placed orders with the old vendor, allowing your old orders to trickle in gradually until all have been fulfilled, at which point your business with the old vendor will cease. (In the latter scenario, you should agree ahead of time to cancel or transfer unfulfilled orders that reach a certain age—one year, for example.)

Switching approval-plan vendors or subscription agents is more difficult, because both involve ending a set of ongoing services with one vendor while essentially duplicating those services with another. In this case, a more appropriate analogy would be trying to change the course of a river. Luckily, in both cases the vendor will usually shoulder the most difficult work. Most approval vendors can translate their competitors' profiles into new profiles for you—though a vendor switch provides a good opportunity to review and rewrite completely your old profiles, and it will often be a good idea to do so. Similarly, your new subscription agent will usually offer to manage the details of transferring subscriptions from your old one for you. You will still have plenty of behind-the-scenes work to do, of course, but you will not have to contact all the individual magazine and journal publishers yourself.

14.4 LEAVING YOUR BRIDGES INTACT

If you decide to cease doing business with one vendor in favor of another, you should take care to handle the process with tact and discretion. Unless you are leaving the old vendor because of illegal or grossly unethical conduct on its part, be careful not to bad-mouth that vendor in any public forum. Even if you feel that you have been badly treated by the old vendor, avoid making rash or spiteful comments to the vendor's reps that might make it difficult for you to reestablish a relationship later if necessary. If your new vendor goes out of business or turns out to be worse than the one you left, you may find yourself back with the old one—and thoughtless comments made earlier may come back to haunt you. If one of your professional colleagues asks why you switched, answer directly and honestly, giving a fair assessment of the vendor's strengths and weaknesses. If you are tempted to respond with an axe-grinding tirade, resist that temptation; what your colleague really needs to know is the factors you considered in making your decision.

15 DEALING WITH UNSOLICITED MATERIALS

Every library will, from time to time, receive materials in the mail which it has not ordered or requested. Usually these are innocuous—they may be unsolicited gift books from a donor or publisher, or perhaps sample issues of a new journal or magazine. Sometimes, however, the sender's intention is to trick you into paying for something you did not order. If you are an acquisitions, serials, or collection development officer, your library is counting on you and your staff to be on the lookout for such scams and to ensure that they do not succeed. In this chapter we discuss some typical publisher scams and some proven strategies that will not only prevent tricksters from succeeding in cheating your library—they will also make you a less attractive target and reduce the number of companies making such attempts.

15.1 WHAT YOU SHOULD BE WATCHING FOR

Publishers that engage in this kind of activity usually take one of four approaches, all of them designed to coerce payment by means of guilt, threat, or deception (and sometimes all three):

1. **The Blind Shipment.** In this case, a book arrives with an invoice and a cover letter inviting you to examine the book and, if the book is found desirable, to pay the invoice. Otherwise, you are asked to return the book, usually within thirty days. Often (but not always) a prepaid shipping label is provided.
2. **The "Confirmation" Phone Call.** This one is a common ploy of unscrupulous directory publishers. A vendor rep calls you on the phone, wanting to "confirm your shipping address" or "confirm the information in our directory." You confirm that the information in their database is correct, and two weeks later you receive a copy of the directory in which your entry appears—along with an invoice for

Four common scams:

- The Blind Shipment
- The "Confirmation" Phone call
- The Artfully Ambiguous Solicitation
- The Automatic Standing Order

what is usually a ridiculous amount of money. In some cases, all you will receive is an invoice with a note explaining that you are being charged for your directory entry.

3. **The Artfully Ambiguous Solicitation.** In this case, the vendor sends something that is actually an invitation to order its product, but is deliberately formatted in such a way as to look like an invoice for an item that you ordered. When you receive an invoice that does not cite a purchase order, look carefully at the small print. It may say something about the fact that it is actually an invitation to order or an order solicitation.

4. **The Automatic Standing Order.** This one is relatively subtle, but quite effective. You order the 2002 edition of *Guide to Social Welfare Agencies in California* direct from its publisher. The book arrives several weeks later. A year after that, the 2003 edition arrives unbidden. You call the publisher and say, "We didn't order the 2003 edition." The publisher responds, "This title is one which we automatically supply on standing order."

The follow-up to each of these is often **The Legal Threat:** once the invoice begins to mature, you start receiving threatening letters promising dire legal consequences if payment is not immediately forthcoming. Interestingly, the very threatening tone of these letters can serve as a useful tip-off regarding the company's legitimacy. In general, honest companies do not try to secure payment by frightening your staff. Instead, they send a couple of invoices and then follow up with a courteous and professional phone call. Scam vendors, on the other hand, tend to start in early with threats of collection proceedings and legal action. This is a technique designed to subdue critical thought—the vendor does not want you to examine the legitimacy of its claim; it wants you to say, "Yikes! Better pay this invoice right away before my staff and I all get thrown in jail."

Of the approaches listed above, the **Blind Shipment** is the least objectionable, in that the vendor is at least being up-front about the nature of the shipment and is not trying to fool you into thinking you have ordered the item in question. However, it is still technically illegal and it is a practice you would be wise to discourage—on top of all your other duties, you and your staff do not need publishers sending you unsolicited books that you will have to distribute within your library for consideration and keep track of, only to have to return them later.

Publishers that employ the **Automatic Standing Order** gambit are not necessarily trying to cheat you; although in some cases the practice is a conscious attempt to trick you into buying something you do not want, in others the vendor is genuinely trying to provide a service—if you want this year's edition, the logic goes, you will probably want next year's updated edition as well. But good intentions on the publisher's part do not make this practice acceptable; the publisher needs to offer you a standing order, not impose it on you.

If you receive an **Artfully Ambiguous Solicitation** in the mail, contact the sender immediately and let the person you speak with know that you do not wish to receive any such notices again, and that if the vendor continues to send them it will run the risk of legal action. A vendor that wishes to offer you a product by mail should send an informational flyer or brochure, not a solicitation that is designed to deceive your staff into paying for something that was never ordered.

The **"Confirmation" Phone Call** is the most sinister of these gambits; in this case, the vendor is trying consciously to deceive you. Worst of all, the vendor in this situation will often target an employee from outside the acquisitions or serials department—preferably a student employee or someone who is not trained to recognize scams.

All of the above approaches share one thing in common: in each case, the vendor is trying to get you to buy something by putting it into your hands and hoping that inertia, guilt, or intimidation will lead you simply to pay the invoice and be done with it. In each case, paying the invoice is the path of least resistance, and these vendors have learned that librarians and their staffs respond no differently from anyone else to the charms of that path.

> *Rule of Thumb: As a matter of course, all staff and student employees in your library should refer calls from publishers or vendors to the acquisitions or serials department—especially if the vendor is asking to confirm the library's shipping address.*

15.2 IF YOU DID NOT ORDER IT, IT IS YOURS

The good news is that United States law is very clear about the status of unordered merchandise: if a vendor or publisher sends you materials that you did not order, those materials are yours to do with as you see fit. Here is the full text of the relevant section of the law (U.S. Code Title 39, Section 3009):

> Except for free samples clearly and conspicuously marked as such, and merchandise mailed by a charitable organization soliciting contributions, the mailing of

unordered merchandise or of communications prohibited by subsection (c) of this section constitutes an unfair method of competition and an unfair trade practice in violation of section 45(a)(1) of title 15.

Any merchandise mailed in violation of subsection (a) of this section, or within the exceptions contained therein, may be treated as a gift by the recipient, who shall have the right to retain, use, discard, or dispose of it in any manner he sees fit without any obligation whatsoever to the sender. All such merchandise shall have attached to it a clear and conspicuous statement informing the recipient that he may treat the merchandise as a gift to him and has the right to retain, use, discard, or dispose of it in any manner he sees fit without any obligation whatsoever to the sender.

No mailer of any merchandise mailed in violation of subsection (a) of this section, or within the exceptions contained therein, shall mail to any recipient of such merchandise a bill for such merchandise or any dunning communications.

For the purposes of this section, ''unordered merchandise'' means merchandise mailed without the prior expressed request or consent of the recipient.

> **Rule of Thumb:** If someone sends you something you did not order, it is yours to do with as you wish.

There is very little ambiguity here: if a publisher sends you a book (or lists you in its directory, or starts sending you issues of its journal) without asking you first, you are under no obligation to pay for that item or service, nor do you need to return the item to the sender (even if the vendor sends a prepaid shipping label).

15.3 WHAT IF THE VENDOR DID TALK TO SOMEONE IN MY LIBRARY?

This is a legitimate question. In some cases, the vendor may really have received a phone request from someone in your organization and there may be no order record in your system to reflect that. Presumably, your procedures are clear and intelligent enough to make that very unlikely. But if you suspect that such might be the case, take a moment and send an e-mail out to the library staff, asking whether the title in question rings a bell with anyone. If someone did call and request the book, you have a training issue, and maybe a procedural one as well. (Telephone orders are sometimes necessary, but they should always originate in the acquisitions or serials department, and they should always be reflected by an order record in your internal system—regardless of whether an actual purchase order was sent to the vendor.)

In very rare cases, you might suspect strongly enough that the phone request really happened that you decide to go ahead and pay the invoice. But you should think carefully before taking that course of action. If the argument between you and the vendor really comes down to "they said, we said," then the burden of proof is on the vendor, not you—it is up to the vendor to prove that the order happened, not to you to prove that it did not. That may seem cold and legalistic, but imagine what would happen if you made a habit of giving vendors the benefit of the doubt in situations like this one. Anyone could claim to have received an order from you and you would have no way of knowing whether it were true. When a vendor responds to an order and does not keep records sufficient to substantiate that order later, the vendor has made a mistake—and absorbing the consequences of that mistake is the vendor's responsibility, not yours.

15.4 STANDING UP FOR YOURSELF: A MODEL

If a vendor insists that you have ordered an item and your records indicate that you have not, you need to find out why the vendor thinks you have. This means establishing three things:

1. Can the vendor cite a purchase order that you can verify in your records?
2. If not, can the vendor tell you who he or she spoke with at your institution?
3. If not, can the vendor provide any substantiation at all for its claim? (Anecdotal reports are not sufficient—if it cannot be faxed to you, do not believe it.)

Here is how the conversation might go:

Librarian: I'm calling to find out why we received this directory. I'm sure we didn't order it.

Vendor: Actually, you did. We received the order on January 23.

Librarian: Can you tell me what purchase order number we used? I can't seem to find the order in our records.

Vendor: We didn't get a purchase order; we took the request over the phone.

Librarian: Can you tell me the name of the person who requested it?

Vendor: No, we don't keep track of the names of everyone we talk to on the phone.

Librarian: I can understand that, but you need to appreciate my position: without a purchase order and without knowing who you talked to, I can't confirm that we really did order this.

Vendor: Well, it's too late to return it now. You had thirty days, and the deadline has passed.

Librarian: That's where you're mistaken. Unless you can provide me with evidence that we actually ordered this book, we're under no obligation to pay for it—or even to return it. According to Title 39 of the U.S. Code, Section 3009, we can treat unsolicited merchandise as a gift. That's what we're going to do in this case. Of course, if you can demonstrate that we really did order this book, we'll gladly pay the invoice.

Vendor: All right, all right. We'll make an exception this time and allow you to return the book.

Librarian: No, you don't understand. By law, the book is ours. I'm not going to invest the staff time necessary to package and return it. I want to discourage you from doing this in the future, and the best way I can think of is to keep the book and not pay the invoice. Hopefully this will convince you to take us off your mailing and phone solicitation list.

SAMPLE LETTER IN RESPONSE TO AN UNSOLICITED SHIPMENT:

Dear Sir/Madam,

We have received from you a book that we did not order, along with an invoice; please find a copy enclosed. It appears that it was sent to us in hopes that we would wish to purchase.

This marketing tactic is illegal. In accordance with Title 39 of the U.S. Code, Section 3009 (the full text of which is attached), we will treat this book as a gift, and we will either keep or dispose of it as we see fit. We will do the same with any unsolicited materials you send us in the future. This includes updates of books that we may have purchased in earlier editions.

You may feel free to continue sending us free books if you wish. Be advised, however, that we will not pay for books we have not ordered, nor will we invest the staff time necessary to return them to you, even if you provide postpaid shipping labels. You would probably do best to cease sending us unsolicited materials and to desist from establishing standing orders for us without our consent.

If you have any questions or concerns, please feel free to contact me.

Best regards,

(signature)

15.5 SHOULD YOU EVER GIVE IN?

There is a very good reason for being as hard-nosed as possible with vendors who are trying to cheat or manipulate you: the best way to discourage an unscrupulous vendor from targeting your library again in the future is to make doing so as unprofitable as possible. Saying "I'll pay the invoice this one time, but this had better not happen again" is not very effective. It is much better to say, "I will not pay this invoice, nor will I return the item." This approach causes the vendor's scam to backfire immediately and makes it clear that they cannot push you around.

However, there may be circumstances in which you want to give the vendor a break. If the vendor is a reputable one, with which you have had a constructive relationship in the past, or if you are convinced that the unsolicited shipment was an honest mistake, or if there is some other reason to believe that the vendor undertook this course of action in good faith, you should consider returning the item (at the vendor's expense, of course). As important as it is to be firm with those who are trying to cheat you, it is equally important to extend professional courtesy to those who may have simply made an honest mistake. You and your staff will likely make mistakes in the future, and you will want your vendors to extend that same courtesy to you.

16 WORKING WITH PROBLEM VENDORS

In Chapter 14 we discussed reasons for switching vendors and techniques for doing so effectively and professionally, and in Chapter 15 we discussed ways of dealing with vendors who are actually dishonest or unethical. In the former case, the problem is one of extricating yourself from a vendor relationship that has gone bad, and in the latter it is one of being on the lookout for scammers and con artists who will actively pursue your library, trying to cheat you.

In this chapter we focus on what can be, ultimately, a still more difficult problem: dealing with vendors who stay on the right side of the legal and ethical divide, but whose practices make it difficult or unpleasant to do business with them. Where those difficulties are not serious enough to lead you simply to cease doing business with the vendor, or where their services are essential to your library and its patrons, you will need to be prepared for the particular challenges that the vendor is going to present you. In this chapter we discuss some of the more common challenges you will be likely to face, and some strategies for dealing with them.

16.1 DEFINING THE PROBLEM VENDOR

One of the difficult things about being a librarian is the fact that you are not a completely free agent in the marketplace. Like someone who lives in a town with only one poorly-run gas station, you will at times be forced to do business with people whose practices you find objectionable or whose prices are unreasonable. For example, if your library serves a school of veterinary science and the core journal in that field costs more than you think is reasonable, you will probably have to swallow your professional pride and subscribe to it anyway. Similarly, if a very powerful professor on campus insists that you simply must maintain a standing order for a series published by an imprint with a terrible reputation for service, you will probably simply have to deal with the terrible service. You may want to try to talk the professor out of that standing order, but if she sticks to her guns, chances are good that you will have to go along with her. This is an example of when

(see sidebar)

WHY WON'T YOU GIVE A LIST OF SPECIFIC VANITY PRESSES?

No publishers, even those that seem most unapologetically engaged in vanity publication, appreciate being referred to as "vanity presses." In addition, some publishers occupy a sort of shadowy territory between legitimate and vanity publishing. To avoid unwanted consequences for my publisher (Neal-Schuman), I must refrain from naming any such presses here. However, a quick Internet search using phrases like "vanity publishing," "vanity presses," "self-publishing," or "publish your book" will yield quite a bit of useful information. The Internet has unfortunately led to a proliferation of vanity presses, but it also offers an effective resource for identifying and avoiding them.

monopoly power works against the library; if only one publisher is selling the content and you must have the content, then you will have to take it on the publisher's terms.

Luckily, this is not always the case, and it is almost never the case with service providers (such as booksellers and subscription agents), most of which are selling their services in a competitive marketplace. It is usually, though not always, possible to avoid doing business with vendors whose practices you find objectionable or whose service quality is not up to your standards.

Examples of typical "problem vendors" include the following:

- **Vanity presses.** Vanity presses (also known as "subsidy presses") publish books based not on their quality or salability, but rather on an author's willingness to subsidize the publication process in whole or in part, or on the author's willingness to forego royalties entirely in return for uncritical acceptance of his manuscript. Some of these presses make money by charging their authors exorbitant amounts; others do so by representing their books to the academic community as serious scholarship and counting on librarians not to pay very close attention to the content of those books. Not everything that comes from a vanity press will be worthless, of course, and there may be occasions when a vanity press publication is actually an essential purchase for your library. But these presses, and their products, should be regarded with deep suspicion.

  While offering a list of vanity presses themselves would be problematic here (see sidebar), there are certain characteristics of presses and their books of which you should always be wary:

  a) **Charging authors directly.** While it is fairly common for scholarly journals (especially in the hard sciences) to impose "page charges" on authors, the practice of charging the costs of publication to authors is unusual in the monographic world, and should be taken as one indication that you may be dealing with a vanity press.

  b) **A defensive tone in its promotional literature.** A press that "protests too much" about the scholarly nature of its list is one that should be regarded with a skeptical eye. Legitimate scholarly publishers do not waste a lot of time telling you how scholarly

Telltale signs of a vanity press:

- Charging authors directly
- A defensive tone in its promotional literature
- A stated focus on "speed to market"
- Cageyness about editorial practices
- Unusually high list prices

their books are; they assume that you understand that they are scholarly publishers and they advertise their books based on the books' and authors' individual merits.

c) **A stated focus on "speed to market."** Watch out for publishers that trumpet their ability to publish books within months of manuscript acceptance. This is usually the sign of a publisher that invests minimal effort in the preparation of its publications.

d) **Cageyness about editorial practices**. One hallmark of vanity presses is that they leave all editorial work to their authors, requiring them to submit "camera-ready manuscripts." This means that there is essentially no quality control—no one employed by the publisher to look over the manuscript for typographical errors, no one fact-checking, or doing any of the editorial work. Usually a quick glance at any book published in this manner will make clear the folly of such an approach.

e) **Unusually high list prices.** There are, of course, many legitimate publishers that charge high prices for their titles. But the combination of unusually high prices with some of the other red-flag indicators listed above should be taken as one more warning factor.

- **Vendors without domestic offices.** Vendors and publishers that do not have offices in your home country will always be more difficult to deal with than those that do.

Rule of Thumb: A company that has struggled financially in the past will struggle financially in the future. Radical financial turnarounds can happen, but they are not as common as bankruptcies.

- **Vendors with a history of financial instability.** It is true that companies, like people, are capable of changing. It is also true that the best predictor of the future behavior of companiesis their past behavior. In other words, a vendor that has a checkered financial past is almost certain to have a checkered financial future, and while you may not be able to avoid doing business with vendors in that situation, you would be wise to take the past into account when deciding whether or not, for example, to establish a deposit account with a particular vendor.

- **Vendors with a constantly changing sales force or executive staff.** Companies that cannot retain sales

Examples of problem vendors:

- Vanity presses
- Vendors without domestic offices
- Vendors with a shaky financial history
- Vendors with a constantly-changing sales force or executive staff
- Vendors that lag behind the competition technologically
- Vendors that cannot take criticism

Rule of Thumb: A vendor that cannot take criticism is one which places more value on its self-image than on the quality of its services and products, and it is one that cannot be expected to change very much in response to the needs of its customers.

reps or executive-level managers are probably not run well at the highest level, and poor upper-level management will affect everything the company does. Again, you may have little choice but to work with a company that is poorly managed, but you should keep the fact of such management in mind as you are making decisions about how and how much to work with that company—and, of course, as a point of comparison with its competitors.

- **Vendors that lag behind the competition technologically.** Especially in the book business, certain publishers and vendors pride themselves on taking a warm, human, low-tech approach. Many of us in the library profession may find such an attitude refreshing and even charming, but a company's low-tech approach will usually cost you money in the long run. A company that does not use e-mail (or whose employees use it badly), that does not have a well-designed and well-supported web site, or that does not have a computerized system of invoice generation and account maintenance is one that will end up wasting quite a bit of your and your staff's time.

- **Vendors that cannot take criticism.** Unfortunately, you probably will not find out that a vendor takes criticism badly until your relationship with the vendor is well under way. But while it may be awkward, it is almost never too late to stop doing business with a vendor, and any time you find that your complaints and suggestions to a vendor are met with excuses, sob stories, or anger, you should seriously consider doing just that. Do not be too hasty to judge an entire company based on the behavior of one employee, of course, but be alert to signs of a corporate culture that is based on defensiveness.

16.2 HOW CAN YOU AVOID THEM?

In many, though certainly not in all, cases it is possible to avoid doing business with problem vendors. When you are choosing between vendors, you have several resources to help you research and compare them.

- **Your colleagues.** The easiest and most reliable way to find out about a vendor's competence and service quality is, of course, to talk to that vendor's existing customers. It is essential that you talk to more than just those to whom the vendor itself refers you. It is also important, however, that you conduct your inquiry with a certain level of professional discretion. Do not issue a blanket question on a public discussion list, inviting participants to offer their opinions of the vendor in that forum. Except in rare and severe cases of incompetence or unethical behavior, criticism of a vendor should take place in a more private venue.

- **Better Business Bureau.** The Better Business Bureau offers a searchable website at http://www.bbb.org. Here you can check to see whether formal complaints have been lodged against the vendor you are considering doing business with; you can also register complaints against vendors with which you are having problems.

- **Listserv archives.** While it is not usually appropriate to initiate critical discussion of vendors in a public forum, such discussions do take place from time to time, and the online archives of such lists as ACQNET, SERIALST, COLLDV-L and LIBLICENSE-L can offer useful information. Those archives can be found at the following URLs:

ListServ	URL
ACQNET	http://www.infomotions.com/serials/acqnet/
SERIALST	http://list.uvm.edu/archives/serialst.html
COLLDV-L	http://www.ala.org/alcts/cmds/colldv-l.html (offers instructions on searching the archives by e-mail)
LIBLICENSE-L	http://www.library.yale.edu/~llicense/ListArchives/

- **Google.** Of course, there is the ever-popular practice of "Googling"—entering the name of the vendor in question as a phrase in Google and seeing what turns up. This will actually uncover comments that have been made in various e-mail discussion groups, as well as formal press releases and other public statements. In many cases there will be so many instances of the vendor's name online that your results will be too numerous to be useful. However, you can limit the results to those most likely to be relevant by adding search terms like "service quality," "problems," and "service issues."

When you find potentially useful information from any of the above sources, of course, you should take care to consider the reliability of each of them. Is the librarian that you talked with someone whose judgment you know to be sound? Is the web site that you found in the course of your Google search one that was established by a competitor or someone else with a clear axe to grind? Who issued that posting to ACQNET? Where the substance of a criticism can be confirmed or debunked by querying the vendor, take the time to do so—for example, if someone criticized a book dealer for not offering shelf-ready services, but the criticism was registered in an online discussion that took place three years ago, check to be sure it is still accurate. Where criticisms cannot so easily be substantiated or debunked, be cautious and critical in your acceptance of the opinions offered.

16.3 WHEN YOU MUST DEAL WITH PROBLEM VENDORS

When you have no choice but to do business with a vendor with whom it has been difficult to work in the past, or that you have good reason to believe is going to be difficult to deal with in the future, you have a few strategies at your disposal to help minimize those problems.

- **Be direct and straightforward about the vendor's failings.** Take opportunities to remind the vendor that its services are not what they should be, or that its responsiveness leaves something to be desired. Your comments should be delivered in a courteous and professional manner, but do not soft-pedal your criticisms; it is in no one's interest for the vendor to

When you must deal with a problem vendor:

- Be direct and straightforward about the vendor's failings.
- Let the vendor know its performance is being watched.
- Offer to be bought off.
- Threaten judiciously.

maintain the illusion that it is providing good service when it is not. By the same token, when improvements are forthcoming you should be equally ready to let the vendor know that you have noticed and appreciate them.

- **Let the vendor know that its performance is being watched.** Most vendors care what kind of service they are providing their customers, and if you let them know that you have been dissatisfied with them or that others have warned you about certain aspects of their service, and that you will be watching their performance closely, this will almost always result in improvements. Consistency over time is important when taking this approach; do not let your guard down because things go well for a month or two. When service degrades, let the vendor know promptly and politely. When promised upgrades do not materialize, ask for an explanation and do not allow yourself to be easily mollified by evasive or non-specific answers. And if a particular customer service or sales rep is not responding appropriately to your queries or requests for service, ask for a new one.

- **Offer to be bought off.** If a vendor cannot provide you a desired service, ask what it will do to make it up to you. For example, if the vendor has an unwieldy and out-of-date online ordering system, ask for an enhanced discount (to make up for the extra staff time that will be needed in order to deal with it), with the understanding that your discount will revert to its previous level if and when the vendor institutes specific improvements. (Will this gambit always work? No. But at worst, it will give you one more way of registering your displeasure with the vendor's failings and will position you as a reasonable customer who is willing to make compromises.)

- **Threaten judiciously.** In cases where you actually do have some degree of choice in dealing with a particular vendor, do not hesitate to threaten to take your business elsewhere if service levels drop below acceptable standards. In many cases this is the single most effective way to bring service levels back to where they should be. Consider the experience of one serials librarian:

When I arrived at my new job and began taking an inventory of our current vendors, I quickly realized that our subscription agent had been virtually ignoring our library for about a year; there had been no visit from a sales rep and no significant effort on the agent's part to check in with us and see how we were doing and whether their services were meeting our needs. And this despite the fact that we were doing about a quarter of a million dollars' worth of business with them every year! I immediately contacted the vendor, asked who our sales rep was, and told them that I was seriously considering giving our business to one of its competitors, since they obviously didn't care one way or another whether we remained as their customer. The result was almost instantaneous. My sales rep came to visit within the week and worked very hard to regain our trust and goodwill. We ended up not only rebuilding a very good relationship with that vendor, but also negotiating a reduction to our service fee. The agent has remained responsive and helpful to this day, and at this point I would not even consider switching to another one.

Of course, you will not always have the option of threatening your vendor with a switch to the competition. But even where you have little choice but to stay with the vendor, telling the vendor that you are going to begin seeking out competitors and looking for ways to get the services you need that do not involve that vendor will likely have a similar effect.

- **Public shaming.** This is a strategy that should be used rarely and only in the event of significant ethical lapses or severe and sustained incompetence. In such cases, you might consider sending a message to a public discussion group explaining your problem and asking others whether they have had similar ones, and what they did to solve them. This can be helpful in several ways: for one thing, another library may have found someone at the vendor who is particularly helpful or may have found a way around the problem you are having. For another, there is a good chance that the vendor's reps monitor that discussion group and will be stirred to action by public discussion of its failings. Sometimes the threat of such public discussion may be enough to stimulate the vendor; consider sending your rep an e-mail message that says "Since my repeated attempts to get an answer to this question have failed, I'm going to bring this up as a discussion topic on SERIALST and see whether any of my colleagues have been more successful in getting answers from your company." If you still get no response, you will at least be able to tell the rep that you gave her fair warning before taking your criticism of her company public.

17 UNDERSTANDING THE ETHICS OF VENDOR RELATIONS

It is probably safe to say that librarians are not, generally speaking, people who have been propelled into their profession by cutthroat business instincts. We are not generally here to leverage our capital or diversify our holdings or maximize the bottom line. In fact, many librarians would probably confess that they find the business world foreign and maybe a bit distasteful, and that their choice of profession reflects that feeling. Instead of joining the corporate rat race, they deliberately chose a profession that would allow them to concern themselves with serving the academic world or the general public.

This is, to be sure, a noble sentiment, but it holds potential pitfalls for the librarian. One is the pitfall of naïveté—the possibility that, by turning up his nose at the business world, the librarian will fail to understand those with whom he does business, and end up making unwise decisions and potentially losing or misspending his constituents' money. Another is the pitfall of simpleminded scorn for the world of business, which can lead to the belief that, since he is working for the public good, anything the librarian does in the interest of his library and its patrons is morally justified. (You can hear this line of reasoning being implied when a librarian says something along the lines of "Publisher X is gouging us anyway, so it doesn't really matter if we...")

Librarians need to develop a certain amount of sophistication when it comes to business ethics and practices, especially since they may sometimes stand to benefit personally from their interactions and relationships with publishers and vendors. The ethics of such situations can be complicated, and deserve careful attention. Obviously, it would be wrong to accept a cash bribe or kickback from a publisher or vendor in return for your library's business. Luckily, such temptations are relatively rare. But most librarians who work in the acquisitions, collection development, or serials areas will be invited out to lunch or dinner by sales reps on a regular basis. Is it ethical to accept such invitations? How about T-shirts, coffee mugs, and tote bags? How about free trips to visit and tour your vendor's corporate headquarters?

In order to sort out questions such as these, it is important to consider two different constituencies to whom librarians have a primary ethical duty. First, toward their patrons and sponsoring institutions; second, toward the vendors with whom they work. In this chapter we examine some general principles of ethical behavior in both of these areas, and then take a detailed look at the *Statement of Principles and Standards of Acquisitions Practice* adopted in 1994 by the Association for Library Collections and Technical Services.

17.1 YOUR ETHICAL DUTY TO YOUR PATRONS

Librarians have many ethical duties toward their patrons—they need to maintain fair and balanced collections, safeguard patron privacy, avoid discrimination in providing services, and so much more. But how does your ethical responsibility in regard to patrons inform your dealings with vendors and publishers?

First of all, your dealings with publishers will have a great deal to do with the ultimate shape and flavor of your collection. If you favor one publisher over another unfairly—for example, a publisher of books with a left-wing political bent over a publisher of right-wing books, or of books with a particular religious message—your collection could easily end up becoming a propaganda tool rather than a balanced information resource. Second, when you deal with vendors and service providers, you have an obligation to marshal your resources carefully, because your resources are not really yours—they are your patrons'. You have a duty to your patrons to make wise and well-informed decisions about the disposition of those funds, which means choosing products and services that will provide the best value for money. (Of course, that may not always mean picking the cheapest product or service.) You should avoid any situation in which your personal interests might get in the way of selecting what is best for your patrons.

17.2 YOUR ETHICAL DUTY TO YOUR VENDORS

Dealing fairly with vendors is more than just a way of ensuring that you do right by your patrons; it is also an ethical responsibility in itself. As an acquisitions, serials, or collection development librarian, you are working in both the library world and the commercial marketplace, and you must hold yourself to the same standards of honesty and integrity that you expect from the vendors with which you do business. At a minimum, this means honoring your contractual commitments and obeying the law. You must, for example:

- Pay invoices on time (or make other arrangements with the vendor)
- Adhere to applicable laws and regulations regarding RFPs, bids, etc.
- Avoid conflicts of interest
- Honor the terms of license agreements and other contracts
- Represent your institution truthfully in regard to size, enrollment, and other particulars.

But ethical behavior means more than just abiding by the letter of the law. It also requires you to avoid "sharp practice," which means the attempt to gain the advantage in a business relationship by underhanded or unscrupulous means, even if those means are not technically illegal. Examples of sharp practice might include the following:

- Sharing confidential information about a vendor with its competitor
- Exaggerating the effects of a budget cut in order to get a deeper discount
- Deceptively encouraging one vendor in order to goad another into offering better terms
- Exaggerating the effects of a vendor error in order to elicit undue restitution
- Spreading ill-founded or unsubstantiated rumors about a vendor's financial status or reliability

In short, dealing ethically with vendors means more than just acting within the law—it means treating them honestly and fairly, even when it would technically be legal to do otherwise.

17.3 THE ALCTS STATEMENT OF PRINCIPLES AND STANDARDS

In 1994, the Association for Library Collections and Technical Services (a division of the American Library Association) adopted an official *Statement of Principles and Standards of Acquisitions Practice.* It is not formally binding on any individual librarian, of course, and the degree to which you adhere to the principles and standards in this statement may vary somewhat depending on your situation. It does, however, serve as a set of useful guidelines when dealing with vendors:

ALCTS STATEMENT OF PRINCIPLES AND STANDARDS OF ACQUISITIONS PRACTICE

In all acquisitions transactions, a librarian:

1. gives first consideration to the objectives and policies of his or her institution;
2. strives to obtain the maximum ultimate value of each dollar of expenditure;
3. grants all competing vendors equal consideration insofar as the established policies of his or her library permit, and regards each transaction on its own merits;
4. subscribes to and works for honesty, truth, and fairness in buying and selling, and denounces all forms and manifestations of bribery;
5. declines personal gifts and gratuities;
6. uses only by consent original ideas and designs devised by one vendor for competitive purchasing purposes;
7. accords a prompt and courteous reception insofar as conditions permit to all who call on legitimate business missions;
8. fosters and promotes fair, ethical, and legal trade practices;
9. avoids sharp practice;
10. strives consistently for knowledge of the publishing and bookselling industry;
11. strives to establish practical and efficient methods for the conduct of his/her office;
12. counsels and assists fellow acquisitions librarians in the performance of their duties, whenever occasion permits.

It might be helpful to look at the elements of this statement individually, and discuss some of their ramifications for day-to-day acquisitions and serials work. According to the statement, a librarian:

"Gives first consideration to the objectives and policies of his or her institution." This means that when dealing with vendors, you put the interests of your library and its users first. You do not allow, for example, a personal friendship with one of your sales reps to influence your decision when making decisions about how (or whether) you will work with that vendor. Nor do you allow your personal political, social, or religious beliefs to determine what you purchase for your library's collection; you adhere to the collecting policy set for the institution by those in authority to do so—though you may, of course, work to influence the shape of that policy. In other words, you give business to (or withhold business from) a vendor or publisher only when doing so will further the specific mission of your library—not because you like or dislike the vendor in question. The first question you ask yourself when making a decision about a vendor is "Will this course of action further the goals of my library?"

"Strives to obtain the maximum ultimate value of each dollar of expenditure." This is fairly self-explanatory; it means that when making purchasing decisions, you consider carefully whether your decision is the one that will do your patrons the most good for the least money. Usually, this means seeking out the best price for a product or service—though you should be careful not to confuse price with value. There will obviously be times when you choose to pay more for a product that is superior, or if you have reason to believe that a particular vendor will save you money in the long run by providing more reliable or responsive service.

"Grants all competing vendors equal consideration insofar as the established policies of his or her library permit, and regards each transaction on its own merits." Some libraries have great leeway in the methods and procedures they may use in selecting vendors. Others are governed by strict legal regulations or institutional rules (such as giving first priority to local businesses). Within the rules that govern your situation, though, you should take great care to offer all interested and competing vendors the same opportunity to offer their services. This does not necessarily mean inviting all vendors to come give a presentation, and it certainly does not mean that you will necessarily end up spreading your business evenly around the marketplace. But it does mean that when you are considering establishing a new service, you should go to the effort of seeking information about as many vendors as you reasonably can, and that you should evaluate that information dispassionately. Early in the process you will likely be able to eliminate some vendors and services that are clearly a poor fit for

Four ways to "work for honesty, truth and fairness in buying and selling":

- Support honest vendors and let them know that their honesty is one reason you support them.
- Confront vendors whose practices are dishonest or unethical.
- Encourage honest and ethical behavior in your colleagues.
- Exemplify honest and ethical behavior in your own business dealings.

your library's needs; the remainder should be offered a fair shot at winning your business.

"Subscribes to and works for honesty, truth and fairness in buying and selling, and denounces all forms and manifestations of bribery." It goes without saying that a librarian should never accept any kind of direct bribe, kickback, or any other kind of payment from a vendor in return for special treatment or consideration. Beyond that, librarians can "work for honesty, truth and fairness in buying and selling" by supporting those vendors they know to be honest and above-board in their dealings with libraries, by actively confronting those vendors whose dealings are not fair or honest, by encouraging ethical and fair-minded behavior in their colleagues, and, not least, by exhibiting such behavior in their own dealings with vendors and other librarians.

"Declines personal gifts and gratuities." This issue is closely related to that of bribery. What makes it complicated is the fact that vendors regularly distribute incidental promotional items like pens, mouse pads, tote bags, T-shirts and bookmarks during conferences or library visits. While this has been a controversial topic for the profession at times, it is generally agreed that the responsibility to decline personal gifts and gratuities does not extend to incidental give-aways such as these. (To test that hypothesis, attend any library conference and count the number of librarians wandering around with vendor-branded tote bags stuffed with pens, mouse pads, bookmarks, and more tote bags. The consensus on this score will be quite clear.)

CAN I ACCEPT ANY KIND OF PAYMENT FROM A VENDOR?

The ethics of accepting direct payments from vendors is somewhat complicated. In academia, it is common for professors to serve on the advisory boards of commercial and non-profit companies and to work independently as consultants to companies and to other academic institutions. Academic librarians—many of whom are part of their institutions' academic faculty—are usually free to do the same, and some of them serve on vendors' and publishers' advisory boards and as members of ad hoc advisory groups of various kinds. The rules that govern public and school librarians' ability to do so will vary from state to state and system to system. If you receive an invitation to serve as a paid member of such a group, make sure you know what regulations govern your participation before you accept. There are some who feel that such participation is inadvisable even where it is allowed. This, obviously, is a personal decision.

Some institutions and states have strict rules about when and whether a vendor may take librarians out for lunch or dinner, but for most librarians, the decision about whether to accept such invitations is a personal one. Some argue that being treated to a meal is no different from any other kind of gift, and that librarians compromise their professional objectivity by putting themselves in that situation. Others feel that there is no ethical issue here; being taken out for a meal is simply a natural part of working with vendors, and the practice is so common that it does little or nothing to privilege one vendor over any other in the librarian's mind. Unless your choice in this matter is limited by law or institutional policy, it is one you will have to make yourself.

"Uses only by consent original ideas and designs devised by one vendor for competitive purchasing purposes." The phrasing of this item is a little bit vague. It refers to the fact that when a vendor is in a competitive purchasing situation (such as responding to an RFP—see Chapter 4), it might share with the library plans or designs for a new service or product that it plans to roll out in the future. The vendor would do so, obviously, in order to enhance its competitive position. It would be unethical for the library to share such information with the vendor's competitors without asking permission first. Now, the line between what can ethically be shared and what cannot is fuzzy—for example, if one vendor tells you that it can arrange spine labels on its processed books in a particular way that fits your needs, there is no reason not to ask a competing vendor whether it can do the same. But applying spine labels is an example of a well-established service that just about everyone knows libraries want, and that most vendors offer. Where you are clearly dealing with a new and original idea, or an innovative design or service, the ethical thing to do is ask permission before sharing that information with a competing vendor.

"Accords a prompt and courteous reception, insofar as conditions permit, to all who call on legitimate business missions." To some degree, the author of this book contradicts or qualifies this item by suggesting, in Chapter 11, that a moderate lack of promptness can be a valuable tool in establishing a power imbalance, and also by suggesting that you should be less than receptive to vendor reps who show up at your office unannounced. Some librarians receive unannounced visits from vendor reps happily; others (including this author) actively discourage such visits. What you do in your own circumstances is entirely up to you and your professional judgment, of course—though it should go without saying that, even when you are telling a vendor rep that you will not see her without an appointment, you should do so politely and professionally.

"Fosters and promotes fair, ethical, and legal trade practices." In what ways can a librarian foster and promote fair, ethical, and legal trade practices? One obvious way, as mentioned above, is by giving

Examples of "sharp practice":

- Sharing confidential information about a vendor with its competitor
- Exaggerating the effects of a budget cut in order to get a deeper discount
- Deceptively encouraging one vendor in order to goad another into offering better terms
- Exaggerating the effects of a vendor error in order to elicit undue restitution
- Spreading ill-founded or unsubstantiated rumors about a vendor's financial status or reliability

Rule of Thumb: Get to know the book and serials business just as well as you would expect your vendors to understand the library profession.

Rule of Thumb: Don't knock efficiency. When we waste time or money, we are hurting our patrons.

business to those vendors that clearly operate within the spirit, as well as the letter, of the law, and who consistently show good faith in their dealings with libraries. In your communications with these vendors, make it clear that one reason you choose to work with them is their honesty and integrity. This will not only let them know that their fair practices are appreciated; it will also give them pause in the event that they consider engaging in practices that are less than fair or ethical. Imagine a meeting in which a vendor's employee suggests that the company could likely get away with a slightly underhanded policy, and another responds quickly by saying, "No way. I hear from our customers over and over again how much they appreciate our honest and above-board dealings with them, and we'll lose much more than we'll gain by abandoning that approach and tarnishing our reputation."

Of course, another, less pleasant way of fostering and promoting fair and ethical business practices is to make a stink about it when a vendor behaves in an unethical way. Sometimes it is our duty as librarians to do just that. Suggestions for appropriate ways of doing so are given in Chapter 16.

"Avoids sharp practice." As discussed at the beginning of this chapter, "sharp practice" means seeking the upper hand in your dealings with a vendor by unscrupulous or unethical means. Not only is it our job to discourage such practices among vendors—it is also our job to avoid engaging in them ourselves, and to discourage them in our colleagues.

"Strives consistently for knowledge of the publishing and book-selling industries." As librarians, we have a responsibility to understand the marketplace in which we work—both the legal realities that govern our interactions with vendors and the economic realities that govern the information marketplace in general. In part, this is simple common sense; we will work better with vendors if we understand the context in which they do their work. But it is also an ethical duty. If we are not informed about the larger information economy, we will serve our patrons poorly. We may allow unscrupulous vendors to take advantage of us, or we may waste time on ill-informed disputes over economic issues, or we may simply fail to find those deals and alliances that will best serve our patrons. Just as it is essential for vendors and their employees to understand the library profession, so it is essential for librarians and frontline staff to understand the book and serials markets and the larger information economy.

"Strives to establish practical and efficient methods for the conduct of his or her office." Efficiency sometimes gets a bad rap among librarians. We generally see ourselves as public servants, and we recognize that what seems like the most "efficient" way of doing things will not always be the way that most benefits those we are here to serve. Efficiency is for managers and accountants, we sometimes think—for those worried about keeping things lean and maximizing the bottom line. If we feel that way, however, we will end up serving our patrons badly. Because efficiency, which really means organizing your work and spending your budgets in such a way that patrons gain the most possible benefit, is what we should all be striving for and it is what our patrons expect of us. Efficiency does not mean that we find the quickest solution to every problem; it means that we find the most cost-efficient way to achieve the best solution. This means that sometimes we will trim down our work flows, if we can do so in a way that does not jeopardize patron service. It also means that we might spend an hour on the phone, if that is what it takes to solve a problem—and if the problem is significant enough to justify an hour on the phone. In all cases, it means that we constantly evaluate whether the result our patrons are getting is worth the time and effort we are investing in it, and whether we might more profitably be spending our time and energy doing something else instead.

"Counsels and assists fellow librarians in the performance of their duties, whenever the occasion permits." As librarians, we have a professional obligation to offer advice, counsel and warning to each other and to share information about practices that work (and about those that do not) as well as about our dealings with vendors and publishers. There are times, of course, when "the occasion does not permit": we need to be careful to keep our information-sharing within the bounds of legal and ethical behavior. It would not be acceptable to share confidential information about a vendor with other librarians, and certainly not with other vendors. However, we do have some control over when information becomes confidential. As discussed in Chapter 7, for example, we should not usually agree to keep pricing and license terms confidential, and most vendors will agree to strike such language from license agreements when pressed.

FURTHER READING:

Nagel, Lawrence. "What Color Is Your Hat?: Ethics in Library-Vendor Relations." *Against the Grain* 14 (2002), 69.

Flowers, Janet. "Ethics Within the Serials Family." *Library Collections, Acquisitions and Technical Services* 26 (2002), 449.

Briscoe, Georgia K. "The Dilemma of Publisher Giveaways." *Against the Grain* 13 (2001), 24.

CONCLUSION

After all of the specific advice, the checklists, the Rules of Thumb and the references to federal law and to official professional pronouncements, the bottom line of vendor relations remains a fairly simple one: be assertive in standing up for yourself and your patrons, and be reasonable in your expectations and treatment of your vendors. You owe it to yourself and your staff (and especially to those who pay your salaries and supply your materials budgets) to make sure that your library funds are well spent. This means doing your homework, seeking out those vendors that will give you the best value for money, and arranging your work flows in the most efficient and effective manner. It also means insisting that your vendors provide an adequate level of service, that they conduct their business with you honestly and ethically, and that they provide the products and services you have purchased in a timely way.

You owe it to your vendors—many of which share your dedication to the world of learning and information, and most of which are operating on relatively thin profit margins—to gain a basic understanding of the information economy and of the environment in which those vendors work, to conduct your business dealings with them in an honest and ethical manner, and to figure out ways that you and your staff can make it easier for them to serve you well. A balanced willingness to stand up for your rights and to recognize your responsibilities will lead you and your staff to build relationships with vendors that are pleasant, fruitful, and mutually rewarding.

APPENDIX A
RULES OF THUMB

- Use e-mail rather than the telephone as often as you can, and if possible, set your e-mail system to automatically archive messages that you send. A searchable archive of your sent messages can sometimes be a life-saver.

- The customer is sometimes wrong.

- Do not do things that will make your vendor want to say "no."

- If you are nice, people are more likely to assume that you are competent.

- Every minute you spend learning your vendor's jargon will result in five minutes saved in your subsequent dealings with that vendor.

- Respond to all vendors' voicemail and e-mail messages within 24 hours, even if you do not yet have a complete answer to the vendor's question

- Never hit <send> until you have reread your e-mail message at least one time through and double-checked the "To" field.

- If your RFP requires vendors to do the impossible, then only liars will respond.

- Every minute spent double-checking arrangements before the vendor's onsite presentation will save twenty minutes of frenzied activity during the presentation.

- When hosting RFP presentations, have more technical help on hand than you think you will need; it may just be enough.

- Good vendors thrive on thoughtful criticism; bad ones resist and resent it. A vendor that cannot take criticism is one which places more value on its self-image than on the quality of its services and products, and it is one that cannot be expected to change very much in response to the needs of its customers.

- If the meeting takes place in the library, someone from the library must be in charge.

- Time with your sales rep is precious and should not be wasted.

- The more decisions you can make before your sales rep's visit, the more productive that visit will be.

- Remember the Gas Theory of Meetings—every meeting will expand to fill the time allotted, and a meeting for which no time limit is set will expand infinitely.

- You will get a discount for ordering books through a vendor, and you will pay a service fee for ordering subscriptions through a vendor.

- The more business you do with a vendor, the less it should cost you.

- Do not pay a renewal invoice that arrives more than sixty days before the actual renewal date.

- Legally, the license means what it says, not what you and sales rep agree it "really means." If you cannot agree to the terms as written, do not sign the license.

- If the license is important enough to the company that you have to sign it in order to get the product, then it is important enough to negotiate.

- Always start with the Good Faith Assumption. Adjust your assessment as the evidence warrants.

- If your vendor will not tell you what is going on, then you can be sure that what is going on is not good.

- If your vendor will not talk to you, then you can be sure that things are going on that it does not want to talk about.

- Any company that makes outgoing calls to ask for your money but will not accept incoming calls once it has your money is not a company with which you want to do business.

- Every company (and every library) will give you a runaround sometimes. Companies that turn the runaround into an art form are hoping that you will simply give up and let them keep your money.

- Legitimate vendors and publishers start out polite, and do not get nasty or threatening until all other approaches have failed. Vendors or publishers that are trying to cheat you will resort to threats immediately, in the hope that you will respond to those threats without looking very hard at the merits of their case.

- Make the format of your purchase orders as boringly consistent as possible.

- Every order you submit, whether by phone, mail, e-mail or electronic interface, should be reflected in your system by a purchase order record.

- If you want the right answer, ask the right person.

- At a minimum, you and your staff should check e-mail several times a day, morning and afternoon.

- You should let your sales rep sell, and your sales rep should let you say "no."

- Exhibit halls are a great place to hear about upcoming products or releases, and a good place to give feedback on broad service or content issues. They are not a good place for long meetings.

- Think such things as your orders, claims, and phone calls, as "outputs" and your vendor as the "customer" for those outputs.

- A vendor that aggressively pursues new customers without proportionately increasing its staff will provide progressively worse service to its customers.

- The basic unit of time in a claiming period is usually one month; claims are usually submitted after thirty days, forty-five days or sixty days.

- Keep a record of noteworthy interactions with your vendors—both positive and negative.

- No good vendor will promise more than it can deliver. If a promise sounds to good to be true, it is probably an empty one.

- You will never switch from an imperfect vendor to a perfect one; you will only trade one set of strengths and weaknesses for another.

- It is always easier to start doing business again with a vendor you have temporarily suspended than it is to get your money back from a crooked one.

- As a matter of course, all staff and student employees in your library should refer calls from publishers or vendors to the acquisitions or serials department—especially if the vendor is asking to confirm the library's shipping address.

- If someone sends you something you did not order, it is yours to do with as you wish.

- A company that has struggled financially in the past will struggle financially in the future. Radical financial turnarounds can happen, but are not as common as bankruptcies.

- Get to know the book and serials business just as well as you would expect your vendors to understand the library profession.

- Don't knock efficiency. When we waste time or money, we are hurting our patrons.

APPENDIX B
GLOSSARY

Acquisitions. In the broadest sense, the term acquisitions may be used to refer to all library processes that involve the ordering and receipt of materials for the collection. In common usage, however, the term usually refers to monographic acquisitions (the ordering and receiving of books), as distinct from serials work.

Approval Plan. An arrangement between a library and a vendor whereby the vendor selects newly-published books according to a set of criteria defined by the library, and sends those books to the library "on approval," meaning that the library staff is allowed to select from among them and return to the vendor those books that they do not wish to keep for the collection.

Backorder. When a vendor has no more of copies of a book or other item in its local stock, it will register your order for that item in its system as a "backorder," which will be fulfilled once stock is replenished.

Blanket Order. This term usually refers to an arrangement made between a library and a publisher whereby the publisher sends all of its new books to the library without awaiting specific orders for them.

Cancellation. In the monographic realm, a cancellation is the repeal of an order. In the serials realm, it usually means the cessation of a subscription or standing order.

Claim. In the monographic realm, a claim is a notice sent by the library to the vendor, asking why a book that was ordered has not yet been received. In the serials realm, claims are sent when periodical issues or series volumes are late.

Claiming Schedule. Claims will be sent according to different schedules, depending upon the nature of the order and the nature of the item expected. For example, a library might claim on a firm order if the book in question has not been received within sixty days of the original order—unless it was ordered from a foreign vendor, in which case the library might wait ninety days. Monthly magazine issues might be claimed when they are forty-five days late, and weeklies when they are fourteen days late. Claiming schedules vary widely by institution and by category of publication.

Claim on Approval. This term is sometimes used to describe a library's request that a specific book be included in an approval shipment, regardless of whether it fits the library's approval profile. A book requested in this way may then be considered for acceptance or rejection according to the same terms as those governing the receipt and rejection of other approval books. It is not a "claim" in the usual sense, since it does not arise out of the vendor's failure to fulfill an order in a timely way.

Competitive Purchasing. This is a generic term used to refer to purchases that "go out for bid," meaning that the library sends out a document to various vendors in which it outlines the service it needs and invites those vendors to compete against each other to win the library's business. Some libraries are required by law or institutional policy to use competitive purchasing practices when the purchase will mean an ongoing expenditure of significant amounts of money. (See also *Request for Proposals.*)

Conflict of Interest. A conflict of interest arises when a librarian's personal interests (financial or otherwise) become entangled with those of either a vendor or his library. For example, a librarian who is related to the owner of a publishing company might be said to have a conflict of interest in his dealings with that company. Not all relationships that pose potential conflicts of interest are significant enough to merit serious concern, but some governments and institutions require their employees to report and document all potential conflicts of interest, no matter how minor.

Consortium. A group of libraries that agree to cooperate in a formal way on any number of possible projects. Most commonly, libraries band together to form consortia for the purpose of maximizing cost and labor efficiencies when making large purchases of online databases, journal content or books.

Coverage. A vendor's ability to obtain the materials you need from a wide variety of sources. A vendor that can sell you books from two hundred publishers offers greater coverage than one that can only sell you books from one hundred publishers. (Coverage should not be confused with *Fulfillment*, which refers to a vendor's speed, accuracy, and completeness in responding to your orders.)

Customer Service Rep (Representative). The staff member at a vendor or publisher who is charged with solving problems and meeting your needs on a day-to-day basis. She is different from the *Sales Rep*, whose primary job is to sell you new products and services.

Deposit Account. A fund into which you deposit lump sums of money, and from which you then draw throughout the year rather than paying individual invoices as they are issued. Most vendors offer the option of placing money on deposit with them, and offer interest payments or enhanced discounts in return.

Firm Order. The most common type of library order. This term refers to orders in which the library asks a vendor or publisher to send a specific item. Books sent on approval are understood by the vendor to be sent for consideration and may be returned; when the library submits a firm order, on the other hand, it means that the library definitely wants the book in question. In most cases the library will be allowed to return the book if it wishes, but returns of firm-ordered books should be rare.

Focus Group. Like politicians and marketing agencies, publishers and vendors occasionally pick groups of customers on whom to try out ideas for new products or services, or from whom to elicit ideas and feedback. These are called focus groups, and librarians working in acquisitions, serials, or collection development may be asked to serve as members of such groups from time to time.

FTE. "Full-time Equivalent." The price of access to an online database or service will often be determined, at least in part, by the number of people who will be allowed to use it, so you may be required to report that number to the vendor or publisher of an online product. FTE differs from enrollment (or "headcount") in that it takes into account the difference between full-time and part-time students, counting each part-timer as only a fraction of a full-timer. Thus, a school that has 8,000 full-time and 2,000 half-time students has a headcount of 10,000 (because that is the number of individuals enrolled in the school), but an FTE of only 9,000 (because each of the 2,000 half-time students counts as only .5 FTE).

Fulfillment. A vendor's fulfillment rate is measured by the degree to which it quickly, accurately and completely gives the library what it orders. (Fulfillment should not be confused with *Coverage*, which describes the number of sources a vendor can draw upon to fulfill a library's orders.)

Indemnification. To indemnify someone is, essentially, to agree to serve as that person's legal insurance policy. A library that indemnifies the publisher of an online database against claims brought by third parties arising from the misuse of the database by a patron is saying, in essence, that if a patron uses information from that database to injure someone else, and that someone else tries to sue the database publisher, the library will take the publisher's place in court. Such language is often found in license agreements, and should usually be negotiated out before the library signs the agreement.

Integrated Library System (ILS). An integrated library system is a computer system that coordinates multiple library functions with a single bibliographic database. It will usually be referred to in conversation as an ILS or simply as the library's "system." An ILS is usually comprised of different modules—one for circulation, one for monographic acquisitions, one for serials, etc., thus allowing librarians and staff in different areas to perform different sorts of maintenance tasks on a single database, through different interfaces.

Invoicing Period. The amount of time that a vendor allows to pass between invoices. For most annual subscriptions, the invoicing period is one year; you may be invoiced for online access to a database on an annual basis, or the charge may be spread out over several invoices during the year. This is only an issue for ongoing services—since books are usually invoiced as they are shipped and are paid for only once, there is no "invoicing period" as such in their case.

ISBN. "International Standard Book Number." This is a ten-digit number assigned to a book when it is first published. It is specific to the edition and binding of the book—thus, a reprint will have a different ISBN from the original edition, and if a book is published simultaneously in cloth and paperback bindings, each will have a separate ISBN. On most commercially-published paperback books, you will find the ISBN printed above the UPC symbol on the back cover; in hardbound books, you will find it listed on the verso of the title page, near the Library of Congress Cataloging-in-Publication information.

ISSN. "International Standard Serial Number." The ISSN is an eight-digit number that serves as a unique identifier for series, multi-volume sets, periodicals, annuals, and other serial publications.

Jobber. A wholesaler. Most book vendors that sell to libraries are acting as "jobbers," meaning that they buy books in bulk from publishers and then resell them individually to libraries.

Jurisdiction. Your library is subject to both federal and local laws and regulations. Many license agreements contain language that, if you agreed to it, would make the agreement subject to the publisher's local laws and regulations instead of your own. Libraries that serve state institutions are usually forbidden from agreeing to such terms, because they cannot agree to be subject to the jurisdiction of another state. Even where the library has the option of agreeing to such terms, it is usually unwise to do so. Most publishers will agree either to change the jurisdiction clause so that it refers to the library's local jurisdiction, or simply to eliminate the jurisdiction clause altogether—but the librarian needs to be sure to ask for that change.

Kickback. A payment that a vendor offers you in return for winning the library's business. In a competitive purchasing situation, one of the competing vendors might take you aside and offer to pay you a percentage of the company's net profits from sales to your library if you will, in return, use your influence to ensure that his company wins the contract. That payment would be a kickback. Obviously, kickbacks are both unethical and illegal.

License Agreement. When you purchase access to an online database or to an electronic book or journal, you will usually be asked to sign a contract that defines who may have access to the product and what the library and its users are allowed do with its content. This contract is a license agreement. For a more detailed treatment of license agreements, see Chapter 7.

Listserv. An online discussion group in which participants can share questions and concerns and ask for information. Several that are of particular interest to those working in acquisitions, serials or collection development areas are listed in Chapter 16.

Management Report. A report that shows activity between a bookseller and library on a particular account over a specified period of time. Management reports are most commonly used to analyze the activity of an approval plan, and will usually show how many books have been sent on approval, how many kept and how many returned, among other statistics. Some booksellers allow customers to create customized management reports through an online database and receive them by email or screen display.

Mix. (See *Publisher Mix*)

Monograph. Literally, a monograph is a book on a relatively narrow topic written by a single author. As used commonly by booksellers and librarians, though, the term is generally used simply to mean a book, as distinct from a serial publication.

Non-subject Parameter. In an approval plan profile, non-subject parameters are those aspects of a book that have little or nothing to do with its topic or intellectual content. Date of publication, price, and physical dimensions are all examples of non-subject parameters. (See also *Subject Parameter*.)

Notification Slip/Form. An approval plan profile will generate not only books to be sent on approval, but also notifications of books that are more marginal to the library's interests. The library can then respond to those notifications by requesting them selectively on approval or simply submitting firm orders. Paper notifications may be referred to as "slips" or "forms," depending on the vendor, and are usually available in either paper or electronic format.

OPAC. "Online Public Access Catalog." The means by which patrons look up books, journals, and other library materials to see whether they are held by the library. The OPAC is the electronic version of what was once a card catalog.

Periodical. (See *Serial.*)

Profile. A document that describes the kinds of books that a library would like to receive on approval, as well as those that should be excluded. An approval plan may consist of one large profile or a number of subject-specific profiles. Depending on the vendor and library preference, these may be treated as separate profiles or as subsets of a larger one (referred to as "subprofiles").

Publisher Mix. The diversity of publishers covered by an approval plan is referred to by vendors as the "mix" or "publisher mix." Mix is relevant to vendors because of the variety of discounts that publishers offer them. If the mix of publishers covered by your approval plan is weighted towards those that offer the vendor very low discounts, the discount you receive from the vendor will probably be correspondingly low. If your publisher mix leans toward high-discount publishers, your discount from the vendor should be higher.

Purchase Order (PO). A paper or electronic form used by a library to submit an order to a vendor or publisher. The form that the library sends will have an identifying number that links the order to a record in the library's accounting system; when the book is received, the library can then match it to an order record and confirm that the order was fulfilled correctly.

Renewal. Most periodical subscriptions are renewed annually. Libraries renew their subscriptions either by paying a renewal invoice (usually sent directly by the publisher) or by reviewing a renewal list (usually sent by a subscription agent), indicating whether any of the listed subscriptions should be cancelled before paying the balance.

Request for Proposals (RFP). A request for proposals is a formal tool libraries may use to solicit bids from vendors in a situation that calls for competitive purchasing. The RFP is a document that describes the library's needs and invites vendors to submit formal proposals to meet those needs. From those that respond, the library will usually select a smaller number to come to the library and make a formal presentation.

Sales Rep (Representative). The person who is charged by a vendor or publisher with selling you new products or services and with resolving general questions or concerns about the products or services that you already purchase. In most cases, your sales rep will not be deeply involved with technical or day-to-day problems (those are the province of the *Customer Service Rep*). Rather, the sales rep is more focused on the maintenance and support of the larger relationship between the vendor and your library and with increasing the amount of business your library does with the vendor. Sales reps usually travel extensively, and may visit you on a regular basis.

Serial. A generic term that describes any item that is published in more than one part and that is expected to continue indefinitely. Magazines, scholarly journals, annuals, and conference proceedings are all examples of serials. A periodical is a type of serial; the term usually refers to publications that are issued fairly frequently and regularly, such as magazines and scholarly journals. Sometimes librarians will use the term "periodical" to mean that type of publication specifically, and the term "serial" to mean all other types of serial publication (such as sets, annuals, and ongoing book series).

Service Fee. The charge that is added by a subscription agent to the price of a subscription. This charge covers the costs that the agent incurs in gathering and administering subscriptions on the library's behalf; it is the price you pay for not having to handle hundreds of individual invoices (and deal with hundreds of individual publishers) separately. The larger the number of subscriptions your library has (and the smaller your staff), the more likely a service fee will look like a good investment. Smaller, better-staffed libraries are more likely to choose to handle all of their subscriptions directly.

Sharp Practice. The attempt to gain an advantage in a business relationship by underhanded or unscrupulous means, even if those means are not technically illegal. (See Chapter 17.)

Shelf-ready. Books that are received "shelf-ready" are those that have been physically processed by the vendor to the same extent that they would have been by the library itself, and that arrive with full catalog records that are ready to be loaded into the library's system. The processing might include any combination of the following: spine labels with call numbers, security devices, binding, property stamps, and protective book jackets.

Standing Order. A standing order is something like a subscription, except that it usually involves volumes in series or sets rather than issues of a magazine or journal. A standing order indicates the library's desire to buy all volumes in a particular series as they are published.

Status Report. A report from the vendor to the library, explaining the status of an unfulfilled order. Status reports are generated once an order has gone unfulfilled for a specified amount of time—for books, generally four to six weeks. If the order continues to go unfulfilled, more status reports will be generated until the order is either fulfilled or cancelled. Typical status report messages include "Out of print," "Temporarily out of stock," and "Publication delayed."

Subject Parameter. In an approval plan profile, subject parameters are those aspects of a book that deal specifically with its topic or intellectual content. Depending on the vendor, subject parameters may be defined according to the Library of Congress classification scheme or according to an internally-defined classification system or thesaurus. (See also Non-subject Parameters.)

Subprofile. (See *Profile.*)

Subscription. An agreement to pay a fee, usually annually, in return for delivery of all issues of a periodical that are published during the subscription period. Libraries may make subscription arrangements directly with publishers or through one or more *Subscription Agents.*

Subscription Agent. A type of jobber that specializes in brokering subscriptions rather than selling books. Instead of instituting a hundred individual subscriptions with individual publishers, a library may set up those subscriptions through an agent, thus consolidating the invoicing and some of the management tasks involved in maintaining those subscriptions. A subscription agent will usually charge a fee for this service.

System. (See *Integrated Library System or ILS*)

Unsolicited Mailings. These are products that you have not ordered, but which are shipped to you by a publisher or other vendor in the hope that you will either consider them for purchase or, in the case of less scrupulous publishers, mailings are sent in the hope that you will mistake them for items you have ordered and will simply pay the invoice. According to Title 39 of the U.S. Code, Section 3009, you may treat unsolicited mailings as gifts and are not required either to pay for or return them. (For more details, see Chapter 15.)

URL. "Uniform Resource Locator." This is the unique address assigned to every document that is available on the World Wide Web. It usually begins with "http://www" and will usually end with a category extension, such as ".com" (indicating that the host is a commercial company), ".org" (indicating a nonprofit organization), ".edu" (indicating an educational institution), or ".gov" (indicating a state or federal governmental body). For example, the web site of this book's publisher is found at this URL: http://www.neal-schuman.com.

Vanity Press. A publisher that selects manuscripts based on the authors' willingness to pay the costs of publication or to forego royalties, rather than on the manuscripts' intrinsic quality or marketability. Some such publishers make no attempt to hide the fact that they are vanity presses, while others adopt the trappings of scholarship in order to lure unwary library customers.

Warranty. A warranty is, basically, a promise that has contractual force. If the publisher of an online database warrants in a license agreement that its product will be completely free from defect and will remain accessible without interruption for the entire term of the agreement, then any defect or momentary lapse in service will technically constitute a breach of the contract. For this reason, license agreements rarely include such warranties, though they may describe a reasonable level of service to which the vendor is willing to commit contractually.

INDEX

Account, definition of, 15, 32
Acquisitions, 157
Advisory group, 144
Approval plan, xii-xiii, 15, 27, 30, 32, 44, 53-57, 157
   non-subject parameter, 54-55, 161
   notification slip/form, 55-56, 161
   profile, 15, 30, 33, 162
   subject parameter, 54-55, 164
Assertiveness, importance of, x, 18, 50-51, 61-63, 77, 78, 89, 95
Backorder, 157
Bad Faith Assumption, 69
Better Business Bureau, 133
Bibliographic record, 56
Binding preference, 28-29
Blanket order, 157
Bonding (of vendors), 40
Bribe, 139, 144
Cancellation, 41, 157
Claim, xiii, 15, 32-33, 73, 92, 94, 101-103, 157-158
   on approval, 102
Competitive purchasing, 142, 145, 158
   see also Request for proposals
Conflict of interest, 141, 158
Consortium, 65, 76, 158
Contract of adhesion, 45
Coverage, 104-105, 158
Customer service rep, xiii, 10, 76-77, 91-97, 158
   as internal customer, 91-95
Customer, external, xiii, 91
Customer, internal, xiii, 91-95
Deposit account, 29, 39-40, 159
Discount, xii, 10, 32, 37-41, 57, 65
Discussion group, 3, 133-134, 137, 161
   ACQNET, 133-134
   COLLDV-L, 133
   LIBLICENSE-L, 133
   SERIALST, 133, 137
Efficiency, 146-147
E-mail, xi, xiii, 3-4, 7, 77

Establishing relations with a vendor, x, xii, 27-35
Ethical responsibilities of librarian, x, xiv, 139-147
   to patrons, x, 139-140
   to vendors, 139-141
Etiquette, xi, xiii, 13-14, 66-67, 95-96, 118-119, 145
   telephone, 13-14
Firm order, 15, 27, 32-33, 44, 159
Focus group, 89, 159
Fulfillment, xiii, 10, 99-100, 159
   accuracy, xiii, 10, 99-100
   completeness, xiii, 99-100
   timeliness, xiii, 99-100
Gas Theory of Meetings, 31
Gifts, from vendors, 142, 144
Good Faith Assumption, 16-17, 68-69
Integrated library system, 87-88, 99, 160
International Standard Book Number (ISBN), 73-74, 160
International Standard Serial Number (ISSN), 74, 160
Internet, 3-4
Invoice, 28, 34, 37, 41-43, 92, 103-104, 160
Jargon. *See* Shared vocabulary
Jobber, 5, 112, 160
Kickback, 140, 144, 161
Library directors, and vendors, ix
Library school, as preparation for acquisitions/serials work, ix
License agreement, xii, 7, 45-52, 141, 147, 161
   alteration of terms, 50
   confidentiality, 47, 52, 147
   disclaimers, 49
   indemnification, 48, 51, 159
   jurisdiction, 49, 160
   termination, 49
   user behavior, institutional responsibility for, 48

Lingo. *See* Shared vocabulary
Listserv. *See* Discussion group
Management report, 15, 33, 161
Meetings with vendor reps, 23-32, 34
    agendas, 31-32
    managing, 31-32, 34
    planning, 23-31
Mix. *See* Publisher mix
Monograph, 160
Non-subject parameter. *See* Approval plan
Notification slip/form. *See* Approval plan
Online public access catalog (OPAC), 160
Order record, 125
Order, submission of, xiii, 73-75, 92
Periodical. *See* Serial
Physical processing, 11, 28, 34, 41-42, 44, 56, 105-107, 163
Profile. *See* Approval plan
Publisher mix, 38-39, 162
Punctuality, 80, 83
Purchase order, 73-75, 92, 122, 125-126, 162
Reasonableness, importance of, x-xi, xiii-xiv, 18, 50-51, 61, 64-65, 77-78, 89, 95
Reference librarians, and vendors, ix
Renewal, 10, 162
Request for proposals, xii, 21-25, 27,141, 162
    follow-up, 24-25
    hosting presentations, 23-24
Returns, 10-11, 37, 44, 65, 92
RFP. *See* Request for proposals
Sales rep, xiii, 10, 27-29, 34, 76-77, 79-89, 163
    at conferences, 87-89
Search engine, 6, 134
    AltaVista, 6
    Google, 6, 134
Serial, 15, 33, 42, 163
Service fee, xii, 32, 37, 163
Shared vocabulary, xi-xii, 14-16, 32-34
Sharp practice, 141-142, 146, 163
Shelf-ready services. *See* Physical processing

Shipment error, 17, 76
Shipment schedule, 9-10, 28, 34, 37
Statement of Principles and Standards of Acquisitions Practice (ALCTS), xiv, 140-147
Standing order, 27, 32-33, 163
Status report, 15, 33, 41, 163
Subject parameter. *See* Approval plan
Subscription, 15, 27, 164
Subscription agent, 5, 37-38, 40-42, 63, 93, 100-101, 112-113, 116-118, 130, 136, 164
Switching vendors, 111-119, 129
System. *See* Integrated library system
Terminating relations with a vendor, x, xiv,
Terms of service, xii, 37-44
UCITA. *See* Uniform Computer Information Transactions Act
Unethical vendors, x, xiii-xiv, 17, 69-70, 114
    public shaming of, 136-137
Uniform Computer Information Transactions Act (UCITA), 46-47
Uniform resource locator (URL), 5, 133, 164
Unsolicited mailing, xiv, 63-64, 72, 75, 121-127, 164
    ambiguous solicitation, 122-123
    automatic standing order, 122-123
    blind shipment, 121-122
    "confirmation" phone call, 121-123
    U.S. law regarding, 123-124, 125
Usage statistics, 6
Vanity press, 130-131, 165
Vendor database, 4
Vendor responsiveness, 17, 62-63, 95, 99, 101-103, 117
Vendor visits, preparing for, xii, 29-31, 81-82
Warranty, 49, 165
Windfall allocation, 39
World Wide Web, xi, 3, 7

ABOUT THE AUTHOR

Rick Anderson grew up in Arlington, Massachusetts, and earned his B.S. and M.L.I.S. degrees at Brigham Young University. Before assuming his current position as Director of Resource Acquisition at the University of Nevada, Reno, he worked as a bibliographer for Yankee Book Peddler, Inc., as Head Acquisitions Librarian for the University of North Carolina, Greensboro, and as Electronic Resources and Serials Coordinator at Nevada. He serves on the editorial boards of ACQNET and Library Collections, Acquisitions and Technical Services and on the advisory boards of several publishers and library service providers, and edits the Sound Recording Reviews column for *Notes* (the quarterly journal of the Music Library Association). He writes a regular column for *Against the Grain* entitled "IMHBCO (In My Humble but Correct Opinion)," which tells you something about his personality.